Design / Layout:
Imagine It! Media, Inc.
Palm Springs, CA
www.imagineitmedia.com

Crown Printers
250 West Rialto Avenue
San Bernardino, CA 92408
909 888-7531

Printed in the United States of America

For more information:
www.jerering.com

For Mom...

Acknowledgments

Liberace - what else needs to be said? Ray Arnett for introducing me to Liberace. Joe Hyams for making me aware that I am a writer and telling me to get off my ass and write. Jesika St Clair for her brilliant editing. Patrick Perry for introducing me to Jesika St Clair and answering the phone every time I call. Steve Pettinga for kicking off his low-heeled backless marabou mules and introducing me to Patrick Perry. Jeff Shotwell and his team at Imagine It! Media for bringing my imagination to life. Erin Warren at Crown Printing for her patience, persistence and perseverance. Sue McGrew my favorite biatch who helped me write, organize and create. Johnny Jaqua for putting up with the biatch who showed up everyday (with an obnoxious smile on her face - nobody should be that happy!) who fed us delectable daily dishes and inspired us with his humor and remarkable spirit. Alida Guidry for her support. Jake, Muffy, Jozelle, Scooter, and Daisy for their canine clowning and companionship.

And Mom for being my ever-present spirit guide through this journey.

if the shoe fits
buy two!

For Maggie,
You Gorgeous Dame!
Too Bad I'm Not Three
Weeks Younger!

♡

2018

Table of Contents

PREFACE

Keep the Dream

Master of my destiny … What will be life's gift to me?
Waiting and wondering … Hoping and pondering …
What does my life mean?

I won't fear the dark of night … Meet the dawn and find the light.
Knowing my eyes can see …
All that they're meant to see …
Searching for my dream.

Let me see the sunlight, let the day begin,
Let me know the fullness of my soul within,
Let me see how wonderful my life has been,
Content as I may be.

But, I realize that there is so much more,
When I walk the path that I've not walked before,
On the threshold of another open door,
That leads me to my dream.

Now, I've learned to trust in God to show me the way.
I must spread my wings and soar,
Face up to the sky, I know my heart can fly,
Suddenly, I find that I am seeing a brand new day!

I can feel all the joy that my hope can bring,
As now, I am clearly seeing everything,
Still, I'll never want to cease my questioning,
In search of what life means.

How I love the rhythm of life's poetry,
Of how beautiful the song of hope can be,
As a wondrous world has opened up to me,
The things I've planned are in my hand,
The vision that I've seen,
This is why … I … Must keep the dream!

CHAPTER 1

Something Spectacular!

In 1983, I inadvertently used the power of creative visualization to shape my future. To fulfill a childhood ambition, I set out to become a Liberace protégé. Within months of initiating my crusade, I achieved my goal, and opened the garishly gilded doors to a flamboyant friendship with Mr. Showmanship. By implementing the influence of positive thinking, I truly achieved … *Something Spectacular!*

Lee Liberace, My Glitterati Guru

The press still often refers to me as a "Liberace protégé," even after journalist Forrest Duke designated me a "discovery" in the *Las Vegas Review-Journal* in July of 1983. Regardless of the title, it didn't just fall into my lap. My alliance with Lee (as he was known by close friends and family) Liberace was the consequence of an intricate plan. I had to map out my maneuvers and keep my eye on the objective. Successes in life require endeavor and justly merits reward.

I knew Liberace would become my mentor when I first saw him on stage, at the open-air Starlight Musicals theatre in Indianapolis. I was eight years old and totally enthralled with the enigmatic, glittering piano man. At age eight I decided that I was going to meet him. During the intermission, I excused myself to the boy's room, but bolted off to scrutinize stage doors for backstage access. I finally discovered how to get to him—but it took me nineteen years to do it.

In the early 1980s, I was attempting to acclimatize myself to Los Angeles and the pain of pursuing show business. I had grown weary of getting paid thirty-five dollars per day as an extra on B-rated films: The sting of skinned knees from falling off my skates on the set of *Roller Boogie* was rivaled only by the humiliation of running for my life with hundreds of other scantily clad slaves in *Conan the Barbarian*. I worked as a waiter in a handful of diners and began playing piano in a collection of restaurant-bars. I also began developing a fondness for alcohol. Until I could get a handle on my drinking, I decided to stop working in piano bars and took a menial job as a houseboy for a dubious pair of wealthy gay men in the Hollywood Hills. My days were spent tidying up bedrooms, bathrooms, and living areas that the pair had all but destroyed the previous night.

On one exceptional evening when I was asked to help with a dinner party, I learned that Ray Arnett, Liberace's stage manager, would be one of the invited guests. That evening I prepared a flawless dinner for eight, and while I was clearing plates, I cleverly suggested that the guests enjoy dessert and coffee in the living room … near the piano. Once everyone was knee-deep in peach cobbler, I slipped onto the piano bench and began to play. Just as I anticipated, my playing caught Ray Arnett's attention, and he invited me to lunch the following day.

In the ensuing weeks, Ray and I developed a loosely knit friendship. I joined the gym that he attended, and we began working out together—the nearly forty-year difference in our ages provided a safety net for any misjudgment. We were friends, and that was the extent of it. I took the liberty of asking Ray multitudes of questions about Liberace, and spending a great deal of time at the library reading everything I could about the man: his favorite foods, colors, art forms, destinations, and … well, private proclivities. I read everything I could get my hands on. In early June of 1983, Ray mentioned that Liberace was opening at the MGM Grand Hotel in Las Vegas and asked if I would care to see the performance. Of course I agreed, and arrangements were made; I could feel the momentum building as the days moved on. I continued my vigilant research and creatively visualized myself as the next Liberace protégé. The initial stages of my plan were magically falling into place.

The Hunt and the Chase

My then-partner Dale Brunner and I drove to Las Vegas and checked into the MGM Grand Hotel on the morning of Thursday, June 23, 1983. I remember the date well as it had been logged in my mental agenda for weeks. I had been to Vegas before, but this trip held inexplicable promise, and I nervously anticipated meeting my long-awaited mentor.

We arrived at The Celebrity Showroom with plenty of time to spare and were seated at a large table in the King's Circle. The show was naturally over the top, only with a cheesier Vegas flair. Liberace was obviously in familiar environs. He made his customary stage entrance in the mirrored Rolls Royce Phantom V limousine with Scott Thorson's replacement, Cary James, at the wheel. Pianos gleamed and the dancing waters cascaded as Liberace gushed his legendary clichés to a cheery audience.

When the extravaganza concluded, we met Ray who escorted us to an elevator that was filled with a host of small dogs. We arrived at another level and were guided through a labyrinth of hallways that led to the star's reception room. Upon entering, I was amazed by the size of the space, but disappointed by the large crowd of frenzied fans that waited inside. A small flight of stairs, flanked by pedestals of candelabrum, led up to a pair of ornate doors at the back of the room. As the overhead lights dimmed, rose-tinted spotlights went up, lighting the doors as they opened to reveal Liberace in a gold and red ceremonial Chinese robe. As he descended the stairs, he greeted the adoring crowd with royal gestures and basked in their adulation, greeting, kissing, and embracing them. I stood, waiting in anticipation for my turn to be introduced. Unlike the frivolous crowd, I was there with a purpose. I knew I had to somehow capture his attention, and I was aware that this might very well be my singular opportunity to do so.

As Liberace approached, I mentally rehearsed my lines. If the first one didn't captivate him, I had a backup plan. I spoke confidently as I shook his hand, "I thoroughly enjoyed your performance. I'm going to go home and practice my little fingers off."

He responded with the celebrated Liberace nasal parlance, "Oh, you play piano too, do you?" as someone else grabbed his attention.

Dale and I stood and observed the crowd for some time, until, as people began to leave, he started tugging my arm. "Don't you think we had better leave soon?"

"I'm not done here yet!" I barked.

The crowd finally dispersed, leaving Ray Arnett, Cary James (Liberace's new partner), Seymour Heller (Liberace's manager), Dale, and myself. As we gravitated toward a large L-shaped bar in the corner of the room, I corralled the group into a seating arrangement granting me the greatest conversational access to Liberace. I was successful.

As the group discussed the particulars of the performance, a security guard entered the room with a considerable strongbox that he hoisted onto the bar to my left. Liberace continued chattering as he began individually removing his legendary rings from his fingers, and casually handed them to me to pass along to the security guard.

A chill ran through me as I handled the famous jewels. I could not resist slipping them on my fingers. I was amazed that the diamond-encrusted piano ring he wore on the ring finger of his left hand dangled loosely on the thumb of my right. Just as I slipped the candelabrum ring on, he turned to me and smiled. He reached for my left hand and gently removed the ring to show me that the candle flames were mounted on three sides with marquise-cut diamonds that twirled as he spun them. He placed it back on my finger, and then took the pave-diamond piano ring from me, and opened it to show the tiny golden piano strings inside. He looked at me and smiled.

"They're beautiful, aren't they?"

I glanced at my hands and wondered how many people would love to see the famed pieces of jewelry, and even more so to have them on their fingers. As I handed them to the guard, he placed each one into an individual velvet bag and then into the strongbox.

I determined that it was time to lay the next step of my plan, my trump card.

"I recently appeared on a cruise ship and had the opportunity to read several of your books." I shared this in a quiet voice. It was both flattering and informative: I took the time to read his books, and now he knew that I was a professional performer. I continued, "I particularly enjoyed the story of how you introduced yourself to Nöel Coward on the Queen Mary."

That did it. He spun his barstool to face me, and we began an energetic conversation, his attention was mine! We chatted only a short while before he turned back and told Ray that he would like arrangements to be made to hear me play. I tried to conceal my welling eyes as I became aware that my dream was taking form.

After the plans were made, Dale and I bid farewell to the group and left the dressing room. We were escorted by security to a lower level and directed to a set of fire doors that led to the casino area of the hotel. Amidst clanging slot machines and winners' cheers, I felt my excitement building as we walked the length of the hotel to the wall of automatic sliding glass doors. Exiting the hotel into the sweltering desert heat, I could no longer contain myself. I let out a shout that startled the valets and everyone else within earshot: "I did it!"

When they brought the car around, we sped off into the night … this was only the beginning!

The Universe Works in Mysterious Ways

The universe was smiling on me on Thursday, July 7, 1983, when I ventured to Las Vegas to audition for Liberace. My friend Randy picked me up at the airport and took me to his apartment so that I could rest and "touch up my lipstick" before heading to my much-anticipated shot at stardom.

That afternoon, Liberace and Ray Arnett were waiting for me in the foyer of his Tivoli Gardens restaurant, which he had patterned after its namesake in Copenhagen, one of his favorite international destinations. It was made up of a series of themed rooms that were dazzlingly appointed with a garish assortment of art and antique furniture. A brief tour led us to a concert grand; a mirror-covered leftover from one of his previous shows that found a new home in the piano bar.

I seated myself on the bench and began to play, skillfully weaving one classical theme into the next with sporadic pops of jazz and ragtime. I integrated a cloaked version of Liberace's theme song, "I'll Be Seeing You," before nailing the big finale with "I Love a Piano." Liberace was attentive and courteous. He then invited me to be his guest at dinner at his restaurant, and I graciously accepted. He also let it be known that he was doing two shows at the MGM Grand and asked if perhaps we could connect after the shows, around midnight. This proposition left me somewhat uncomfortable.

As I was enjoying a decadent dinner in the piano bar, Paul Balfour, the scheduled pianist-singer arrived. He introduced himself and immediately began moaning about having to be there. I suggested he slip out the side door, and said I would be happy to tell the management he went home sick. My cunning paid off. I delivered the unfortunate news of Balfour's hasty departure, and restaurant manager Fred Favorite (I love that name) was furious. Joan Rivers, Wayne Newton, and local comedienne Faye McKay had reservations for dinner in the piano bar that night. I offered to step in and cover.

When celebrities appear on the scene, so do the paparazzi and fans. Fred called Liberace's dressing room and left a message asking him to come to the club. Liberace did not waste the time after his show changing clothes, and arrived in full costume. The frenzied crowd nearly blew out the walls when he came to the piano as we played "I've Got Rhythm" in a duet.

That magical night at the Tivoli Gardens will be forever etched in my memory. I had creatively visualized my future and had crossed the finish line. I grabbed the brass ring. I won the lottery. I took a hold of my destiny and wrapped it around my finger. I did what anyone could do, but by damn, *I did it!* I did it! I did it.

My First Reviews

The morning after my night of glory, Forrest Duke wrote my first review in the *Las Vegas-Review Journal*:

"Liberace, noted for his many discoveries including a talented gal named Barbara Streisand, has booked his newest discovery, Jere Ring, for an engagement at Liberace's Tivoli Gardens restaurant. Jere will open his Las Vegas debut on Sunday, July 17, in the piano lounge.

Ray Arnett, who stages Liberace's spectaculars, heard about Ring, a popular performer, and his accomplishments as a piano singer. Ray passed the word on to Liberace who had Jere jet to Las Vegas for an audition. That did it! A new Las Vegas star was born!"

Dick Maurice, entertainment editor for the *Las Vegas Sun*, wrote one of several reviews that I received during my engagement as a Liberace discovery. The exclusive was titled "It's Heaven Playing for Liberace in Sin City" and was featured in his Las Vegas After Dark column. Maurice depicted me as a "vanilla ice cream, hip choir boy" that began playing the piano in church when I was five years old. He was right.

I recall the interview vividly. As I was entering Maurice's condo, John Travolta was exiting. Maurice took a phone call, which gave me a chance to chat with Travolta. He informed me that Maurice was merciless and shrewd. "If he asks you a question, answer it. If you don't, he will answer it for you … in print!"

Travolta was right! Maurice was focused and direct, and maintained a bitter edge, justifying the fact that he had far more enemies than friends. I later learned that in October of 1981, noted psychic Tamara Rand filed a $10 million slander suit against Maurice. He was also targeted for insulting the girlfriend of Gianni Russo, a local Italian gentleman of significance. The girlfriend was Dionne Warwick.

Life with Lee

During my Las Vegas experience, I stayed in one of the many properties that Lee purchased purely for his own decorating pleasure. This particular living space was a holdover from the late '70s. Muted burnt-orange sofas on olive-green shag carpet, and mustard-yellow window treatments accented roughhewn dark-wood. More frightening than the décor was the colony of black widow spiders that inhabited spaces throughout. His signature was inscribed on everything from sheets, hand towels, and throw rugs to dishes and glassware. A colossal autograph swathed even the face of the fridge!

He fancied himself a proficient interior designer (what gay guy doesn't?). But Lee had more dollars than sense when it came to design. Any available space became his palette. One Monday morning, he and I were exploring the back of the Liberace Plaza, when he suddenly shifted into design mode. Off we went on a reckless buying spree for carpets and furniture, and by the end of the week we were arranging silk flowers and fluffing pillows in a secret four-bedroom apartment. He had one party there and rarely returned.

His taste in antiques varied on a scale of goo to extra goo. If it was garishly gilded and unnecessarily impressive, he was writing a check. His intrinsic knowledge of period pieces and their value was limited. A favorite piece in his vast collection of antiques was an exquisite Baccarat Crystal table that was allegedly owned by the Maharaja Bahadur Shah Zafar. Its location altered regularly. Two olive-green Naugahyde La-Z-Boy chairs were flanking the treasure the last time I saw it.

Another day of shopping commenced with a trip to pick up an opal and diamond ring from Barbara Ruffin's jewelry store in the Plaza and continued on to Anna Nateece's fur salon in the Fashion Show Mall where he purchased a full-length lynx coat. By the time we culminated the day, he had a new Rolls Royce and yet another condo. When we returned to his house on Shirley Street, he led me to the backyard where he kept a basket of smooth river rocks and a bag of rubber bands. He affixed his receipts and invoices around a rock with one of the rubber bands and lobbed it over the wall into the yard of Lou Cunningham, his accountant. Once inside the house, he alerted her with a phone call:

"Hi, Lou. It's Lee. Jere and I just went shopping. I left the receipts in your backyard."

The Queen of Bling

He was outrageous, flamboyant, eccentric, outlandish, unconventional, ingenious, ostentatious, and unique. Liberace was the quintessential showman. His motto was, "It isn't done until it's overdone!"

His costumes were elaborate works of art created from silk, metallic, and brocaded fabrics, precious and semiprecious jewels. Furs were added in the last decade of his career and increased the annual maintenance of his costuming to over $250,000. The collection changed with every season of his show; hence, inspiring the reference, "slip into something a little more spectacular." The priciest costume Lee ever wore was an Austrian rhinestone-lined floor-length black diamond mink coat that was worn over a black velvet brocade swallowtail coat. The buttons, platinum-mounted diamonds, spelled his name. Each of his stage creations took around a year to make from conception to completion. With the embroidery and jewelling done by hand, some of them weighed hundreds of pounds. (I know because I was the first performer to wear one of the famed costumes in a public performance when I played for the ribbon-cutting ceremony for the new Liberace Museum on September 29, 1988.)

Lee was clever and innovative. He despised rehearsal, and to avoid the task of preparing new material, he simply embellished the old stuff. By adding more rhinestones, sequins, feathers, and furs, he was able to hoodwink his audiences and dazzle them with illusion. Flamboyantly feather clad, he flew across the stage suspended from a complex rigging system. Upon his landing, he would shed the cape to expose patriotic red, white, and blue hot pants that lit up with hundreds of tiny lights for a grand flag-waving finale.

The legendary jewels that Lee wore onstage were created by numerous designers and composed of the finest stones, platinum, and gold. The entire collection was taken to his personal jeweler for cleaning and securing metalwork about four times per year. His collection was so valuable that when it arrived, the entire store's inventory was moved to a bank vault for storage to avoid superseding limits on the store's insurance. Offstage, the jewelry Lee wore was greatly subdued in comparison. He typically wore a solid gold tailored watch, a small diamond ring, and a large gold coin with a diamond bezel on a neck chain.

The legacy of the candelabra originated at the Persian Room in the Plaza Hotel in New York in 1945. Inspired by the film *A Song to Remember*, he emulated Frédéric Chopin's character and placed a silver candelabrum on the grand piano. The concept took hold. The foundations for his outrageous costuming were established at the Hollywood Bowl in 1952 when he boldly walked onstage in white full-dress tails, making him dramatically distinguishable from the sea of black worn by the 110-member orchestra; he wore a gold lamé jacket in a subsequent performance, and again the concept stuck.

Lee embodied a host of admirable qualities. He also fell victim to his undesirable personal proclivities. His insatiable sexual appetite introduced him to numerous perilous circumstances. He had a propensity for "rough trade" … dodgy sex partners, for those of you who are unacquainted with the term. He always had the net out. While he was in bed with one, he was pursuing another. More than often, threatening bedfellows required ousting by staff, security, or police. He preyed on credulous young men who were easily influenced by dazzling diamonds and the lure of luxury. He had residences in Las Vegas, Los Angeles, Palm Springs, Malibu, and Lake Tahoe, all of which were used regularly for entertaining … of one sort or another.

Beyond the bedroom, Lee maintained a varied social life. He sustained an ever-changing small circle of friends, typically of lesser societal essence. He did not receive invitations from the Rockefellers or the DuPonts, nor did he care to. He also shied away from unknown performance venues. He favored being in control of his environment as opposed to it controlling him. He was not one to take chances for fear of failing. When he found a comfort zone, he remained there.

He had many protégés and upon becoming one, I quickly discovered that the opportunity did not come without negative aspects. Encouraging young talent presented a reciprocal remuneration. Vince

Cardell, one of my more prominent predecessors, advised me to claim the title and swiftly make my exit. If prolonged, the association with the Liberace name could be damning. Adoring fans greatly admired him for generously sharing the stage but the real question was who was using whom? If Lee found no personal reward in the relationship, it would typically be short-lived. Such was his relationship with his mother as well. His unconditional love for Francis was a bogus act, fueled by guilt and responsibility. Lee experienced diverse emotions when his mother died; the most apparent were relief and a newfound sense of liberation.

Most fortunately, he never pursued me sexually. Even at age twenty-six, I moved with confidence, and I sensed that he was put off by my self-assured attitude. He and I became fast friends and shared some wonderfully inspiring moments together. The association has played a major role in my life and career and was more due to my efforts than his. Without a doubt, Lee was focused on one thing ... himself. I quickly learned that Lee helped those who helped themselves.

It wasn't until the final years of his life that he took on Radio City Music Hall, and conquered it admirably. He broke all box-office records with several sold-out engagements. *The New York Times* announced, "Liberace is Here, with His Glitter Undimmed." Shortly after that glowing headline hit the front page, the glimmer faded, and the bling diffused, but the sparkle that rubbed off on me still lingers.

The Final Days

In 1986, Lee returned from Sun City, South Africa, right about the time that I returned from Marbella, Spain. I went to Ray Arnett's garden birthday party on September 17, and sat across the table from Lee. He looked like an old woman. His wig was oversized and misfitted. His face was drawn, and his eyes were sunken, but his voice and attitude were vibrant. He went on to New York that fall to complete his third box-office hit at Radio City Music Hall. According to Ray Arnett, Lee did not alter one detail in his show until the final curtain.

On his return trip to the West Coast, he stopped in Chicago to do the *Oprah Winfrey Show*. Shortly after arriving back on the West Coast, he hosted his last Christmas holiday party. Ray Arnett and I, in a recent phone conversation, noted that party was the last time any of us saw Lee "alive." After that night, he retreated into his Palm Springs home and refused visitors, using a variety of excuses.

On February 3, 1987, Ray called me and said, "If you want to see Lee, you better hurry. He's going fast."

I drove to Palm Springs the following morning, and saw Ray just as he was leaving. "It's a madhouse in there," he said. A crowd of fans and followers filled the streets outside the house.

Once inside, I fell to the back of the line, joining those waiting to see Lee. Not knowing if I would be granted a visit at all, I sat quietly in a hallway until close friends and family had paid their last respects. Gladys, the housekeeper, came over and told me to come into the room where he lay barely breathing. I took his hand and shared quiet words and prayers.

"Let go, Lee. Don't fight it. Just let go …"

I left the room and made my way through the crowd outside. When I found my car, and once inside, I lost it. I had to sit for a while to collect myself before I could begin to drive. It was a solemn journey back to LA. As I drove, I turned on news radio to catch the traffic report.

"News 98 … give us twenty-two minutes, we'll give you the world …"

A breaking report interrupted the regular broadcast: Liberace died shortly after 2:00 p.m.

I looked at my watch, realizing that I may have been the last one to see him.

Museum Opening

Dora Liberace (George Liberace's widow) was appointed curator of the Liberace Museum in Las Vegas. She invited me to play for the grand reopening of the museum on September 29, 1988. I arrived at the museum early that morning to be fitted in one of Liberace's costumes. My mother had flown in for the event, so I took her with me.

When we arrived, they opened the vaults to racks of countless costumes. I tried several on, and each ensemble fit as if it was tailored for me—right down to the shoes. I made my choice, and then found my place on the revolving stage at the center of the museum behind one of the mirrored concert grands. As I twirled onstage, guests mingled and sipped champagne. A member of the press furtively informed me that I was the first to ever wear one of Liberace's costumes in a public performance. While at the piano, a friend of Dora's from Austin, Texas, with big hair and rhinestone glasses made a request and handed me a fifty-dollar bill. As the costume had no pockets, I slid the tip into my left shoe.

Following the ceremony, Dora invited several of us into her office. We sat and reminisced about Lee for almost an hour. When I started to excuse myself to change into my street clothes, Dora told me that I would have to leave the costume in her office.

"Everything is on a timer. The doors lock, and the alarm engages at 5:00 p.m."

Uh-oh. I had packed a black duffel inside the case I brought as I planned on absconding with the costume. Damn! Not only did I not liberate the costume, I forgot the fifty-dollar bill in the left shoe. It's probably still there.

Behind the Candelabra

Scott Thorson was twisted, but his book *Behind the Candelabra*, released in 1988, was spot on! The movie starring Michael Douglas and Matt Damon did not pack the same punch that came out of the printed page. A story often loses depth of personification when translated into film.

I had heard a rumor that Scott was living in Palm Springs, and decided that I would like to meet him. So I contacted my old friend Bob Street, who had introduced Scott to Liberace in the late 1970s. Bob was a member of a surreptitious clique of wealthy older gay gentlemen who lived primarily in the affluent Bird Streets neighborhood of the Hollywood Hills. He was a successful dancer-choreographer who, due to astute investing, became substantially wealthy. I learned of Bob's friendship with Liberace at a holiday party at Bob's house in 1982 when he shared a Christmas card he had received from the master showman, a joyful caricature of Liberace at the reigns of a golden sleigh. I was more impressed with the fact that Bob was on Liberace's holiday card list.

Bob and I developed a friendship in the years following my Las Vegas engagement. I had not been in touch with him for some time, but he was pleased to hear from me and happy to connect me with Scott, who called a few days later. We made arrangements over the phone; he would come to my cocktail hour performance at the Racquet Club, and then we would have dinner. Simple, right? Not quite.

Scott arrived at the appointed time Saturday evening, escorted by his sister. I found it odd that she was dropping him off. Did he not have a license? Maybe no car? I didn't ask. The sister's stay was brief, but before taking leave, she stopped at the piano and whispered, "Don't let him drink" in my ear. As she turned and made her way to the exit, she turned and gave me a confirming glare. My immediate thought was, do I look like a babysitter? He ordered a double Scotch on the rocks before the door had so much as shut behind her.

By the time I played out the hour, Scott was hammered. He had no money, so I paid his tab, and we left. He was much too inebriated at this point to act presentably in any other establishment. Dinner was off. I decided to drive him home. The problem was that I had no idea where he lived and he would not tell me. He kept mumbling, "I want to go to a gay bar … I want to go to a gay bar." So, I took him to a gay bar! I dropped him off on Arenas Road in downtown Palm Springs, and he wandered into the shadows.

The next morning, I received a blistering phone call from his sister. Through waves of tyrannical shrieking, I was able to decipher that Scott had been arrested. And this was my problem, how? The story unfolded as the morning went on: Scott ended up sharing a cab in the wee small hours with a dear, sweet friend and illustrious drag queen Bijou. Madame called me around noon and shared an enormously droll series of events that ended in the inevitable incarceration of Mr. Thorson. Taxi drivers have little to no patience for drunken, belligerent fares, and apparently, Scott's conduct was such that it warranted a 911 call. It gave me great pleasure to tell Sis to get a grip, and lose my phone number.

It wasn't until 2006 that I encountered Scott Thorson again. I had developed a friendship with Nicky Ciampoli, who was working as a personal assistant for Carol Channing. Carol and I knew each other socially and would see one another on occasion. Nick was living with Carol and her husband Harry in a gated community in Rancho Mirage. But alas, the closeness of breathing room became too much to bear for young Nick and he relocated to a small apartment in Palm Springs.

On my initial visit to his new apartment, I gave a hefty knock on the door. My approach was more aggressive than I knew. The door to the adjacent apartment flew open and who would have imagined it would be Scott Thorson. I had heard that he was moving in a sketchy drug crowd, using the alias Jess Marlow, but I was stunned! He was a shadow of his former self: sunken, desperate eyes; pallid skin; and cracked lips that could barely smirk. He didn't recognize me, and I certainly did not want to jog his memory. I had my night of adventure with Scott, and I did not need to step into that thicket of thorns again.

I wasn't surprised when I heard that *Behind the Candelabra* was being made into a movie, and I was curious to see how it would turn out. Bruce Fessier, entertainment editor for the *Desert Sun* newspaper in Palm Springs, contacted me and came to my home to interview me for an article that, much to my pleasing, was printed in *USA Today* as well. I was disappointed in the movie. I don't think that Michael Douglas effectively portrayed Liberace, but Matt Damon did a superb interpretation of Scott.

I did not know Scott Thorson when he and Liberace were in the throes of passion; however, I found myself moving with great discernment with the press in 1983 in the wake of the media blitz on the famed palimony suit. I was blond and young. People often approach me with the question, "I understand you played with Liberace!" I love that open door. I respond with, "Rephrase that, and we'll talk!"

Scott Thorson was young and naïve when he met Liberace. Life works that way. I must admit that I had to giggle when the credits ran at the end of the film. "Scott Thorson now lives in Reno, Nevada." He was living in Reno all right, and it wasn't in "a big house," it was in "*the* big house." I wish him well!

A Liberace Christmas

Christmas was Lee's favorite time of year. He decorated everything down to the blades of grass in the yard. Ornaments hung from tinsel garlands adorning chandeliers and sconces. Gold and silver cherubs, glittering angels, and gold bows trimmed multiple Christmas trees; one in every room. Banisters and balustrades were a favorite target. Thousands of twinkling lights blinked and flickered from anything that would support them.

The last holiday party I spent with Lee was in 1985. A group of close friends were gathered on a December afternoon at his Los Angeles penthouse on Beverly Boulevard. We were transported from the penthouse in a fifty-passenger coach to his residence in Malibu, where a compilation of his TV specials played on the overhead monitors to keep us entertained while we were in transit.

When we arrived at the Malibu house, which like many of his others, consisted of a string of condos that were ineptly connected to create one space, food and drinks were served while modest gifts were exchanged. But one gift, which Lee ceremoniously presented to his manager Seymour Heller, fell on the party like a cinderblock.

Somewhere in their history, Seymour had attempted to pull a fast one on Lee in the midst of an endorsement contract with a large auto company in Dallas, Texas. Two aspects were integrated into the contract: a large sum of money and a choice of any car in the showroom. Seymour negotiated the bucks for Lee, but failed to tell him about the red Ferrari that he chose for himself. Lee knew but kept the secret tucked away for years ... until this party.

Lee handed Seymour three small beautifully wrapped boxes at a precise moment. Everyone looked on with keen inquisitiveness as Seymour opened each in orchestrated sequence. The first box held a Ferrari owner's manual. The second one contained a key chain. The third, a garage door opener. Lee then led the group outside to the garages on the lower level. Seymour nervously triggered the remote and the overhead door raised to expose a red tiny toy Ferrari. Lee chuckled and made his way back upstairs. Not another word was mentioned and no one inquired.

In 2003, I began planning a production called *A Liberace Christmas* that I intended to present at the McCallum Theatre in Palm Desert, California. Ray Arnett was working on production; Raul Rodriguez (famed Rose Parade float designer) consented to do set design; Solters & Digney public relations were handling promotion. The performance date was set for Friday, December 13, 2003. The Liberace Foundation had agreed to donate four costumes for the evening to display in the theatre lobby. I was also granted access to the mirrored Rolls Royce that was used to drive Liberace onstage for the opening of his performances.

All the components were in place for what would have been a spectacular show. The only thing I needed was $120,000. I approached every wealthy individual I knew with my prospectus. At the last minute, in a final desperate attempt, I pursued John Otto, a local wealthy executive whose private parties I had entertained. I brazenly donned rhinestone-embellished white tie and tails and a glittery silver wig into McGowan's Irish Inn in Palm Desert, and interrupted a business luncheon to corner him. His initial reaction was one of amusement. He then gravitated to anger and then to hostility. His unprovoked aggression baffled me until May 2009, when I heard on the local news that he had committed suicide near his home in Palm Desert; it was rumored that he had been the mastermind of a sizable Ponzi scheme that eventually caught up with him.

The production of *A Liberace Christmas* faded into the environs of dispirited dreams, cloaked with diluted memories of happier times now gone with the inspiration of its dramatis personae.

The Legend Lives On

It's been close to three decades since Lee died. I see his pictures on the walls of my office and recall …

… The time a group of us piled into Lee's limousine (the one with the piano keys down the side) and took a trip to Twenty-nine Palms to visit his friend George Cannedy. George was a full-on sissy and an heir to a large fortune. His fondness for a sergeant in the Marines inspired him to buy a cracker-box house in the middle of the desert near the base. George was continually adding on to the house until it was a 14,000 square-foot palatial walled home with an Olympic-sized pool, which was regularly refilled with muscular marines.

Following an afternoon of gushing over the ornate house, we went for a drink at the Jumping Cholla, a former Country Western bar that George had transformed into a splashy disco. The joint was jumping with studly Marines and hose monsters (the local women). A handsome young Marine timidly approached Lee with the request for an autograph. "My grandmother loves you." As Liberace scribbled on a napkin, the young Semper Fi continued, "Mr. Liberace, sir, were you ever in the Marines?" Lee looked up taking in the young man's muscular frame and responded, "Oh … I've been in quite a few of them."

Among Liberace's most admirable qualities was his subtle sense of humor. He spoke in innuendoes with underlying currents that few could recognize. He possessed a keen intuition but many times exercised poor judgment. Ray Arnett observed that Liberace was intimidated in my presence; we were equals. I was not there to be one of his conquests. He never pursued me, and I never felt the need to invite that kind of intimacy into our relationship. Contrary to what people want to hear, Liberace never made a move on me. He did not dare!

The entire musical score to Liberace's theme song *I'll Be Seeing You* was elaborately etched into the molding of the mirrored piano bar where I auditioned for Liberace. He often closed his shows with the familiar melody, and I in turn wish to do the same with my own version …

I'll be seeing you, in all the old familiar places …
Atlantic City and Las Vegas … Tahoe too!
I can say … I did it all! I even sold out Radio City Music Hall!
I raked in real big bucks … but then I died and that just sucks!

I'll say … it's great up here! They couldn't care less if I'm a queer!
I get away with everything! Now it's your turn … Jere Ring!
So, thanks for all your accolades … my fans, you are the best!
As for all you other shits … I couldn't care less!

I still play on my rhinestone grand with bigger diamonds on each hand.
I'm glad my brother George is here and that nagging bitch, my mother dear.
And as I think back through the years there's one thing now, I know …
That I wouldn't change a thing … all the glitter and the bling …
But sadly enough … when ya gotta go … Ya gotta go!

CHAPTER 2

Embrace the Journey

I have experienced almost every imaginable mode of travel. From caribou carts and jeepneys in the Philippines to barging and ballooning in France and riding in rickshaws in Vietnam. I have flown in everything from a reconnaissance helicopter to military transport aircraft to the Concorde. I have always been drawn to the sea. Small ships, tall ships, sailing yachts, motor yachts, fishing boats, and rowboats—if it floats, I'm on it.

I have sailed over fifty ships to hundreds of cities in dozens of countries around the world. I have crossed the Atlantic and Pacific oceans more times than I can recall. I have run aground, abandoned ship, put out fights and fires, and have pretty much endured the maritime challenges of a proper seafaring mate. The satirical side of travel can be as entertaining as it is sometimes harrowing and you never know what to expect when you … Embrace the Journey.

I Have Arrived!

When I decided to make my move to California, my family was in disbelief until I packed my little hatchback Dodge Omni and was ready to roll. The car was so tightly packed that when my mother came out the front door with a jar of Tang in her hand, I told her, "There's no room left!" I can still see her in the rearview mirror, standing in the driveway in her full-length gray cerulean mink coat, waving as I drove away.

The three-day trek across the country was as exciting as it was daunting. Once I arrived in California, I stopped at a trendy novelty shop in West Hollywood to buy a greeting card to send to my parents. I chose a colorful card with an artist's rendering of the sun setting over the Pacific Ocean. Silhouetted palm trees framed the view. The wispy clouds in the sky reflected the vibrant hues of the setting sun. On the blank interior I wrote, "Dear Mom and Dad, I made it to California safely. Thank you for your thoughts and prayers. I love you. Jere."

I couldn't wait for mom to receive the card, to give me a call thanking me for the kind gesture. Several days later I received that call. The voice on the other end was that of a distraught mother. "Thank you for the card. I didn't show it to your dad." When I asked her, "Why?" she said, "Did you look at the card closely?" I still did not understand. Mom responded with two words I never thought I would hear her say. The wispy clouds in the sky spelled "Fuck You."

The Alaskan Fairy Fleet

The inaugural of the *Dawn Princess* emanated from Fort Lauderdale, Florida, and made a Panama Canal transit bound for Los Angeles Harbor. Its twin sister, *The Sun Princess*, had sailed some years prior. To enhance the theme of the twin ships, a contest was held, and one set of twins from each of the fifty United States was chosen to enjoy the voyage as guests of Princess Cruise Lines. The celebrated pairs were renowned for a variety of outstanding achievements: Nine-year-old red-haired brothers from Kansas City were executive chefs in a local restaurant. Tenacious sisters from New Jersey were survivors of the holocaust. A pair of ninety-three-year-old gals had graced the stage of the Ziegfield Follies.

Admiral John Jameson was the commanding officer. He and his wife lived across the hall from me on deck eleven. One day in the corridor, I mistook Mrs. Jameson for a stewardess and asked her for new pillows and a blanket. Later on that evening, I became aware of the reason for her snippy attitude when I was introduced to her at the captain's cocktail party. My embarrassment diminished when I noticed that she wasn't fully dressed. I leaned and whispered in her ear, "I think you forgot your skirt." She was standing in beaded top and a slip. She quickly excused herself, leaving me standing with officers handsomely dressed in formal uniform. I was wearing an embellished captain's jacket. When they asked who I was, I struck a pose introducing myself, "I'm the admiral of the Alaskan fairy fleet!"

The Death March

I was marooned on Corregidor Island. A typhoon had moved into Manila Bay suspending service of the hovercraft from Manila Harbor. Having arrived on a day trip, I had no overnight accommodations on the island and ended up staying the night under a mosquito net in a stilted nipa hut belonging to the island's caretaker. My only way off the island was to be paddled in a banca boat through the shark-infested waters to the tip of the Bataan Peninsula. Once I reached the shore of Bataan, I rode in a caribou cart … motorcycle sidecar … jeepney … a bus filled with chickens and goats … finally ending up on the Manila Express.

The Manila Express moved swiftly along until … the driver

left the bus and went inside his house to have lunch! While he was lunching, I learned from an English-speaking passenger the story of the Bataan Peninsula where thousands of Filipino and American prisoners of war perished in the Bataan Death March. Compared to what they went through, my long journey back was effortless.

The Son of a Preacher Man

The passengers on the Alaskan voyage were predominantly families, senior citizens, and conservative organizations. On the first formal night of the cruise, I invited the cast and dancers of the production show for a drink in the disco. The festive evening went into the wee hours of the morning; we closed the disco around 3:00 a.m. As the crowd disbursed, I noticed a handsome tuxedoed man sitting at the bar. I approached him and introduced myself, initiating a chat. As the bartender announced last call, my new friend asked me if there was another place where we could have a drink. In a sultry voice, I answered, "My cabin."

We went below decks, and a night of wild abandon ensued. As morning light peeked through the porthole, he dressed to leave my cabin. Standing with his hand on the handle of the cabin door, he turned and made an anxious request. "Please be discreet. I am traveling with my wife and two-year-old son … and fifty-two members of my congregation." Pastor Jim returned to my cabin every night after I left the stage. He preceded his 1:00 a.m. arrival with a phone call. Each night, moments of passion were interspersed with illuminating conversation, always with the fervent music of the score from the movie *Titanic* playing in the background. Jim was a product of a strict Christian family, his father being the senior pastor of a prominent southern Baptist church. Pastor Jim's wife was submissively oblivious and devoted. She was obviously unaware of his preferences.

On the last night of the cruise, I was anticipating the pastor's call. I completed my show, returned to my cabin, and put on the *Titanic* CD. When I answered the phone, a whispered voice said, "I'm not going to be able to see you tonight."

"Why are you whispering? Where are you?"

"I'm in the cabin. My wife is sleeping."

Shortly thereafter the phone rang again. Over Pastor Jim's voice, I could hear the familiar ding of the elevator. Again, he apologized. I thanked him and wished him well. I fluffed the pillows, turned off the music, and shut the lights. The silence of the room was broken by a faint knock at the door. When I answered it, there stood Pastor Jim barefoot in a terrycloth robe. This night was different from all the others. Pastor Jim's rapture was so strong that after the culmination of our passion, I had to clean the result of his excitement off of the cabin ceiling. My immediate reaction … "Oh my God."

The final morning, as he left my cabin, I offered to give him my phone number, "Pastor Jim, at some point in the future you're going to need someone to talk to." He refused my recommendation. As he walked down the hall, the music still playing in the background, I said, "Remember the *Titanic*."

The ship disembarked in Vancouver, and I ventured into the city for a day of exploration. On my way to lunch, I stopped by a music store and purchased a new CD of the *Titanic* score. With a simple phone call, I found the address of Pastor Jim's church, and in a plain envelope with no note I mailed the CD. I wonder what his thoughts were when he opened the envelope. I often wonder how and where he is. I always wondered if he was aware "my heart *did* go on."

Where Have You Been?

Antigua, Argentina, Australia, Austria, Bahamas, Barbados, Barbuda, Belgium, Belize, Brazil, Brunei, Canada, China, Colombia, Costa Rica, Cyprus, Denmark, Dominica, Dominican Republic, Estonia, Finland, France, Germany, Greece, Grenada, Guatemala, Haiti, Hungary, Iceland, Indonesia, Ireland, Italy, Jamaica, Japan, Korea, Latvia, Malaysia, Malta, Mexico, Monaco, Morocco, Netherlands, New Zealand, Norway, Panama, Peru, Philippines, Poland, Portugal, Romania, Russia, Saint Kitts and Nevis, Saint Lucia, Saint Vincent and the Grenadines, Singapore, Slovenia, Spain, Sweden, Switzerland, Thailand, Trinidad and Tobago, Turkey, United Kingdom, Vatican City, Venezuela, and Vietnam.

Amsterdam, Athens, Auckland, Avignon, Bangkok, Barcelona, Beijing, Bergen, Berlin, Bologna, Brussels, Bucharest, Budapest, Buenos Aires, Calgary, Cannes, Cardiff, Copenhagen, Krakow, Dubai, Tokyo, Toronto, Dublin, Edinburgh, Florence, Frankfurt, Geneva, Glasgow, Hanover, Helsinki, Ho Chi Minh City, Hong Kong, Istanbul, Kuala Lumpur, Lima, Lisbon, London, Lyon, Madrid, Manila, Marrakech, Melbourne, Mexico City, Milan, Vancouver, Venice, Vienna, Montreal, Moscow, Munich, Oslo, Paris, Perth, Prague, Quebec City, Reykjavik, Riga, Rio de Janeiro, Rome, Santiago, Seattle, Shanghai, Singapore, St. Petersburg, Stockholm, Strasbourg, Sydney, Warsaw, and Zurich. Been der! Done dat!

Fifty-Two Ships

I came to adore cruising early on when Mom and Dad planned thrilling voyages to exotic ports for the family. When I was fifteen, San Juan, Puerto Rico, was a port that I had visited only on the reels of my View-Master. The first ship I ever sailed was Royal Caribbean's *The Song of Norway* in 1971 while it was still in its inaugural year. It had a gross tonnage of 18,000 and carried 724 passengers. It was thrilling! I bunked with my Aunt Thelma in an outside luxury cabin while my brother landed with my folks a few decks below … inside. We sailed out of Miami to Nassau, St. Thomas, and San Juan. The voyage lasted a whole week, which seemed like a lifetime to an aspiring young traveler. Since then, that particular vessel has been realigned, redesigned, and reassigned like a revolving door. *The Song of Norway* became known as the *Sundream*, followed by the *Dream Princess, Dream, Clipper Pearl, Clipper Pacific, Festival,* and the *Ocean Pearl.* In January of 2006, while sailing as the *Dream Princess,* it served as a housing facility in New Orleans for Tulane University students in the wake of Hurricane Katrina. After forty-some-years of noble subsistence, the vessel is now MS *Formosa Queen,* a floating casino in China, which, in my opinion, is better than being in the scrap yard. I would enjoy visiting the ship again someday, and who knows? I very well may.

The *Sitmar Fairwind* was a disaster, a cruise to hell. They fired me for sexually pursuing an American doctor who had reported me to the captain for making advances on him. The scenario was quite the opposite. He wanted me, and I wouldn't give. I filed for defamation of character and after winning the suit, discovered that the talent agent who booked me was skimming from the top of my paycheck *and* taking fifteen percent. I sued her, too … the bitch! It has been rumored that my legal triumphs against the cruise line initiated a domino effect. Shortly thereafter, their business ran aground. Good riddance. Goodbye.

I sailed on eleven of the Holland America ships and aside from the smell of formaldehyde and hairspray I remember some good times. The *QE2* sucked! They should have put "The Love Boat" in dry-dock when the show was cancelled. Windstar ships are a spectacular sail. Sea Goddess ships are elegant and unaffordable … the only ships I've ever sailed that replaced the tin of beluga caviar daily. The *Seabourne Pride* caught fire off the coast of Saint-Tropez. The *Star Princess* hit a rock. And you're going to love this one…

We were approaching Ketchikan, Alaska, on *The Regal Princess.*

As the ship was heading for its mooring, we were caught by a port wind and the bow was uncontrollably headed for a bay of seaplanes. Not being able to control the ship, the captain decided to take it directly into the pier. Upon impact, the century-old wharfs disintegrated, mashed like a piece of soggy old driftwood. The impenetrable bow plowed into historic Sockeye Sam's novelty store. The building began to lean and slowly fell into the street. Local codgers Double D and his friend Peaches vividly recounted, "Mary Lou Higgins who lived next door was showering when the building fell, and ran naked into the street! It was the best day of our lives!"

Jamaican Passport

When Princess Cruises lost my passport my first available option was the American Embassy in Jamaica. I made the two-and-a-half-hour journey across the island from Montego Bay to Kingston, and by the time I reached the Embassy the only one left holding the fort down was the American Ambassador himself.

We filled out the necessary paperwork, and he sent me across the street to obtain a passport photo. Standing on the sidewalk, the only person I found was a Rastafarian pinging away on a steel drum against the backdrop of thick jungle. I skipped across the street, tipped him a buck, and asked him if he knew where I could get a passport photo. He stowed his drumsticks and said, "Follow me, mon."

While he led me down a narrow path into the jungle, I wondered if my life would come to a tragic conclusion on the wrong end of a machete. We arrived at a clearing in the jungle where a folding chair sat on a throw rug in front of a soiled white sheet that hung from a rope tightly strung between two coconut palms. After I was ordered to sit in the chair, the Rastafarian bent down and said, "Smile," exposing the two teeth in his head. He snapped the picture and removed the chip from the camera, handing it to a young boy who had suddenly appeared. The boy dashed into the jungle. My Jamaican photographer friend lit up a fat joint, and moments later the boy returned with two photos. The Rastafarian led me back up the trail in a cloud of smoke. I returned to the Embassy while he returned to his drum.

Istanbul Not Constantinople

I spent the day of my fortieth birthday in the ancient city Ephesus, Turkey. I marveled at the Library of Celsus where 15,000 scrolls were held, and stood at the site of the Temple of Artemis where the Apostle Paul once ministered. After leaving the ancient city, I treated myself to an unearthly experience at the ancient hamam in Kusadasi. I was soaked, soaped, scrubbed, and exfoliated, feeling as though I had been dismantled and reassembled in the Turkish bathhouse. I walked back to the *Royal Princess* in a daze. Following my performance that evening, I went by myself to the bow of the ship as we sailed the tranquil Aegean Sea en route for Istanbul. I had not told anyone that it was my fortieth birthday. As I sat alone under the light of full moon I thanked God for my wonderful life and all the special gifts I had been given.

Whenever I am in Istanbul, I am drawn to the Hagia Sophia and the Blue Mosque. I enjoy meandering about the ancient structures and bravely exploring every grotto and crypt. On one expedition in the Topkapi Palace, I happened onto a sacred shrine where a bearded servant of God was chanting from aloft as wailing and flailing faithful followers passed before a glass case below. Out of curiosity, I fell into queue to observe the contents of the case and discover the cause of all the commotion: a gem-encrusted gold-and-silver vessel that contained a lock of hair from the prophet Mohammed. Just in front of the base of the vessel were his gold-plated footprints.

I backed away and melted into the shadows to watch the parade of passersby. One woman was so overcome with emotion that she went into convulsions and collapsed on the floor. A pair of offi-cial-looking men came in and swept her swiftly through an exit door as the parade continued on. After a short while, I moved on to the next display, which was the gilded right arm of John the Baptist. I was as-tounded to find a Christian relic coupled with sacred remnants of the supreme Islamic prophet, and even more interesting was the position of the fingers of the relic, typical of the Byzantine sign of blessing when pointing to Christ as the Lamb of God. In other words, what is all the religious disagreement about? Why can't we all just get along?

The Turks are very pleasant people. To the naïve tourist, their dark Mediterranean characteristics might appear somewhat sinister, but the only crime I ever witnessed in the region was when a group of green Americans accepted an offer from a local for a group photo with the Hagia in the background. There was much confusion about who would stand where and with whom. When the group ultimately found their places for the pose, they discovered that their newly appointed photographer had disappeared with their pricey camera. Don't blame it on the Turks!

The Grand Bazaar in Istanbul is one of the most fascinating shopping experiences on the planet. The Bazaar consists of over six-ty covered streets that play host to more than 3,000 shops. Between 200,000 and 400,000 people visit the covered market daily. I visited the market in hope to find just one quality souvenir. As one can imagine, the rug vendors are annoyingly aggressive. They tug and pull at you as they frantically prattle on in broken English. I chose one small, shy vendor and followed the young man into his lair. Being quite aware of his good fortune, he summoned a group of boys who collectively presented a large assortment of rugs. I specified that I was interested in a runner, as it would be easier to carry with me. A dizzying as-sortment unrolled from every direction, and I was overwhelmed with the options. When I eventually made my selection, the haggling com-menced: I was offered tea, baklava, and almond cookies. "Please ... sit, sit." More tea. Even more rugs. More tea. Finally, with a dramatic wave of my hand, I presented my American Express Card, and declared that

I was done and wanted to leave. I kept one eye on the guy with my credit card while the rug was being folded, wrapped in paper, and tied with twine. I signed the credit slip, thanked the group, and made my exit. Finding my way out of the Bazaar was more than challenging. Because of evidence of a purchase in hand, belligerent purveyors ruthlessly swarmed. I eventually managed to navigate my way through the maze of streets and escape through the fifteenth century gates and into the congested city streets.

On my walk back to the docks, I crossed the Galata Bridge that spans the Golden Horn, the harbor for Istanbul. I found a bench and sat for some time, copping a high from the fumes of the passing cars, vast numbers of ferries, and commercial and pleasure boats in the busy port below. It truly is something to experience. I have never seen an accident in that harbor. They are all skilled drivers, very lucky, or both.

Back on the ship I unwrapped the newly acquired treasure and laid it in the floor of my stateroom. It measured eleven-by-three feet and was beautifully detailed. It should have cost the equivalent of $700 in Turkish lira, but Turkey was a developing country in 1996. The shops were still using old credit-card slide imprinters. I glanced at the receipt and credit card slip, then took a second look. Something was missing. The vendor failed to imprint my credit card. I looked more closely. No imprint! I considered going back to the little man in the Bazaar, but I could barely find my way out, much less find my way back in. And besides all that, we had already set sail.

That's my kinda shopping. Happy birthday to me!

Digby Goes Overboard

The forty-seven day Grand Circle Cruise on the *SS Rotterdam* was a favorite of seasoned travelers. I joined the ship for a ten-day segment from Acapulco to Lima, Peru. An eccentric pair of men from New York City was traveling with their adopted "son" … a fourteen-inch lifelike doll named Digby.

Digby had his own first-class seat from New York to Los Angeles. He had his own "passport," ship transit pass, and seat at the dining table. The real attention grabber was that the traveling trio sported a coordinated wardrobe. They had identical matching outfits for all occasions: glen plaid slacks, blue blazers, button-down oxford shirts, and black formal wear. On island night, they attended the poolside festivities in matching grass skirts. The disturbing aspect of this family unit was that they truly considered Digby their child.

During the course of our voyage, Digby became quite the celebrity, but to me he was a pain in the ass. His seat at the captain's table conjured up a bunch of pissed-off passengers. As a result, we formed the "Dump Digby Club." I drew up a petition, which was signed by several dozen passengers who were in agreement that Digby had to go. We devised a plan that on a sea day someone in the club would snatch Digby from his special seat at the outdoor cafe and fling his tiny ass overboard. Before we could carry off the dastardly escapade, a sinister spy among us revealed our plot. Our fun was foiled, and I was reported to the cruise director. When I was summoned to his office, I divulged our evil endeavor. When he was able to control his hysterical laughter, the director advised me to "let it go." The "Dump Digby Club" was dissolved, and disenchanted passengers expressed their disappointment.

I heard that Digby is now a successful real estate investor in New York. He still has a standing table at the 21 Club, regularly attends the opera, and is a benefactor of the Metropolitan Museum of Art. Instead of cruising on the *Rotterdam*, he has recently been spotted cruising the gay bars of Hells Kitchen … When I had the chance, I really should have just flung the little bastard overboard!

May I Have a Screwdriver, Please?

On my first transatlantic crossing from Southampton England to New York our passage took us through the North Atlantic. After leaving Reykjavik, Iceland, we met with a tremendous storm. *The Royal Princess* was tossed like a toy in sixty-five-foot waves. We were supposed to be the first passenger ship to ever enter a port in Greenland. Unfortunately when we arrived, most of the port had been destroyed in the storm. All the shops were closed with the exception of one hardware store where I purchased a screwdriver. That evening at the piano, whenever anyone offered to buy me a drink, I would hold up my souvenir and say, "No thanks. I already have a screwdriver!"

My second Atlantic crossing was the cruise from hell. *The Regal Princess* made its way into the harbor in Greenland, and this time I had a real screwdriver, one with a lot of vodka. The frightening event on this voyage was Hurricane Bonnie, and we were delayed entering New York Harbor when the captain had to take us out to sea to circumnavigate the storm. We arrived one day late, battered but unbeaten. Hurricane Bonnie was terrifying but the real storm hit three years later on 9/11. That voyage was the last time that I ever saw the twin towers … I think I'll go have a screwdriver …

Look Before You Leap

We were on a ten-day Caribbean cruise out of San Juan, Puerto Rico. On the fifth day of the voyage, a passenger was reported missing by her distraught husband. The captain ordered a full search of the ship, and we spent the next twenty-four hours circling the seas with the assistance of the Coast Guard. A pair of woman's high-heeled evening shoes were discovered on the promenade deck of the starboard aft. The woman was not found, and the search was concluded.

The following week we repeated the itinerary. While in St. Marten, I returned to a favorite restaurant on the French side of the island. In the midst of lunch, a woman approached me and said, "Are you the piano player from the ship?" I froze when I recognized her as the missing woman from the previous cruise. In desperation to share her story, she took me into her confidence and explained. After she jumped from the deck of the ship, a German diver off the coast of St. Marten discovered her. He plucked her from the water and brought her ashore. In ten days they fell in love. She decided to divorce her husband and to remain on the island with the diver. She took a leap of faith and look what happened!

Death at Sea

I joined the SSC *Radisson Diamond* in Rauma, Finland, while it was still in the shipyard. The finishing touches were being made in preparation for the twenty-six-day inaugural voyage to London. Gladys, an insipid female passenger, became an annoyance to everyone on the very first day at sea. She had a notable phobia for everything from dust on top of the glass atrium elevator to fingerprints on the handrails. She was certain that anything that came from the kitchen would be her last meal. By the third day she was known as everybody's nosey neighbor.

Early one morning, I found Gladys sitting alone on the promenade deck. She initiated conversation, and as much as I tried to disengage she would not cut me loose. I seized an opportunity to stir the pot. Looking from side to side, I embarked on a secret tale.

"Last night" … finger to my lips, shhhhh … "I was walking and saw a Russian submarine pull along side."

Her eyes widened.

"I think they came on board to have tea with the captain."

She leaned in closer and said, "Do you think they're still on board?"

I shrugged my shoulders. "I don't know, but the sub left while it was still dark."

Later that afternoon, I met the cruise director Tony who seemed very upset. When I asked him what the matter was he said, "What the bloody hell is going on, on this ship? Everybody thinks we've been hijacked by Russians."

I stood in silence.

"That fucking bitch from Baltimore is telling everyone that she saw a Russian submarine unload a ton of soldiers on the starboard side of the ship last night. The woman is batty! If I could, I would kill her and throw her overboard myself."

Tony did not have to kill her. Gladys disembarked at the next port.

On a subsequent cruise, Cornelia, an elegant matron from Manhattan boarded the ship with her "hired man." The small Chinese man, Ming, constantly pushed her in her wheelchair. Due to her handicap, she demanded to be the first to access the gangway, the food line, and the front row of every show. Every evening at cocktail hour, Ming parked her directly in front of my piano.

She liked my music, and, to be honest with you, I liked her. Her reason for joining the ship was to spread her husband's ashes on the Bay of Biscay. I was one of the only people on the ship invited to the solemn ceremony. A small group gathered on the aft promenade deck as Ming wheeled Cornelia to the rail. He helped her stand; she opened the urn and feebly attempted to dump the ashes overboard. Just as she did so, a starboard wind hit the side of the ship and carried the ashes in an updraft back onto the deck. The sudden dust storm caught everyone by surprise. The serenity of the event was disrupted with frantic waving hands as people covered their mouths, fluffed their hair, and brushed the ashes from their clothes. Later that night, Cornelia hosted a champagne party in honor of her husband. She lost Ming and the wheelchair and hit the dance floor. Life remains after you dump the cremains!

Killing Me Softly with His Song

The piano lounge on the *Cunard Countess* was intimate and cozy. The piano was surrounded with overstuffed chairs and cocktail tables, where people typically clustered to enjoy afternoon libations during my cocktail hour. One older gentleman arrived every evening, and as I began playing, he settled in with a good book. As he read, his head kept rhythm with my music. By the fourth night of the voyage, he and I had become familiar, greeting one another with a nod. To be honest with you, I would have preferred it if he would have found another location on the ship, like maybe the library, for his reading enjoyment. I was more annoyed than flattered.

One night he nodded off, his book resting on his chest. When I arrived for my second set, I found him still slumbering. Go *sleep somewhere else.* I thought.

I became concerned when I arrived for my late night performance and discovered him in the same position. I stood for a moment and studied him. "Sir," I whispered. Then a little louder. "Sir?" I walked to the chair and stood next to him, sensing that something was terribly wrong. With hesitation I touched his hand. He was dead.

Now when I conclude this story, I tell my listeners, "I went directly to the phone and called ship security. A group of officers came to the lounge to remove the old man and discovered a challenge in doing so. Sometimes when people die they 'let go.' The officers carried him out in the chair … and chucked him right over the side of the ship, chair and all!" My audience gasps in disbelief. Gets 'em every time!

CHAPTER 3

Don't Blink!

It could happen in an elevator or on the sidewalk in New York, on a beach in Hawaii or during a walk in the English countryside. They may be sitting next to you at a dinner party or sipping a martini across the bar. Keep your eyes open and … *Don't Blink!*

Bond, James Bond

My friend Matthew West was a famous Aussie. I never could quite figure out what he did but knew it had something to do with film and television. He often entertained in his gracious home in the Hollywood Hills, preferring formal sit-down dinners and intimate cocktail gatherings. One evening, I was late in joining a spirited group of diners. When I arrived, I found my place at the table and attempted to catch up with the conversation. Matthew was seated at the head of the table of ten and focused much of his attention on a woman seated at the opposite end with a manner as untamed as her spiked red hair. He also shared his attention with the man sitting to my right.

Feeling more comfortable at the edge of the conversation, I studied the faces of guests around the table. As more wine was poured, formalities faded, and the banter began. Just as I became more aware that the woman at the end of the table was the focus of attention, she pulled her leg up to her chest and rested her elbow on her knee—quite a curious pose for a formal dinner. I turned to the guest on my right to inquire who she was. When he turned to face me, I was close enough to kiss … Timothy Dalton. How did I not recognize his profile? Frozen in my chair, I could not speak; I could not eat; and I could not drink. When I came back to earth, I whispered my question.

The woman was Lynn Redgrave.

As Time Goes By

The SS *Azure Seas* was a rust-bucket ship that made three- and four-night runs to Catalina Island and Ensenada, Mexico. Those of us who worked on the ship referred to it as "The Azure Sleaze" or the "Seize Your Ass." So I'm sure that it was purely for convenience that the ship was the floating location for filming the 1980s television special, *Celebrity Fun Cruise*. Englebert Humperdink, Ruth Buzzi, Andy Gibb, and T.G. Sheppard were in the cast. Ruth Buzzi was funny as hell. T.G. Sheppard was … T.G. Sheppard. Englebert Humperdink slouched and was in desperate need of shoulder pads. Andy Gibb was cute as a bug's ear.

One afternoon at sea, I was perched on the piano bench organizing lyric cards. I suddenly felt someone behind me and turned around to find Andy Gibb standing next to the piano. "Do you mind if I sing a tune with ya?"

Of course, I obliged and asked what he would like to sing.

"As Time Goes By."

I struck a chord. He took the microphone and off we went into one of the worst renditions of the classic song that I have ever heard. In a Bee Gees-esque style, he fished for the lyrics: "*You must remember thi-ih-ih-ih-is, a kiss is just a ki-ih-ih-ih-is …* " As I focused on him with narrowed eyes, I noticed movement in my peripheral vision. Much to my amazement passengers began to fill the room.

When I concluded the lackluster performance, the audience erupted with applause. "Are you kidding me?" I thought. "I guess when you look like Andy Gibb, it doesn't matter how you sound." Now he is gone. The ship is gone. But memories linger.

May I See Your Driver's License?

Skip E. Lowe—Hollywood talk show host and author of *The Boy with the Betty Grable Legs*—invited me to be a guest on his show. On my designated day, I was honored to share the interview with classic crooner Rudy Vallée and Susanna Foster, best known for her leading role as Christine in the 1943 film version of *The Phantom of the Opera*.

Rudy was not familiar with the location of the studio, and when he was late for the taping, I volunteered to go outside and keep vigil from the sidewalk. Standing in a vacant parking space at the studio's front door, I spotted Rudy's sputtering station wagon weaving down the street toward me. He pulled up in front of the building. As his car gave a single backfire, a mangy mutt stuck its sleepy head out of the window. From the side of his rearview mirror, I motioned Rudy into the vacant parking space. Just as I gave him the "okay" signal, the car lunged forward and crashed into the vehicle in front of him.

It was my car.

Do You Have an Extra Pillow?

It's an appalling feeling to wake up fully dressed on a couch in a living room of a house that belongs to someone you have never met. But it happens.

I woke up in a strange place and was experiencing the numbness that preludes a throbbing headache. I stood on wobbly legs. As I shuffled, I heard someone stirring upstairs. Soon, the person descended the stairway in the hall and made the corner with a broad smile on his face. He said hello and asked if I slept well. I gave an honest response, "As far as I know."

He told me he had brought down an extra pillow, and then invited me to join him in the kitchen. Through the conversation, I gathered that he was a singer. Comments about my playing the piano the previous night caught me by surprise. Neither did I recall seeing nor playing a piano. According to my host, I must have been good; he raved about how well I had accompanied him. When he said, "There are very few people your age who know that song," I was more than embarrassed to inquire as to which song he was referring.

"The Little White Cloud That Cried."

My host was iconic Johnnie Ray. Later that morning, I sat with him in the bathroom while he had his hair cut and then his hairdresser gave me a ride home.

Can I Hitch a Ride?

Beverly Hecht was a powerful Hollywood talent agent. She was also a bitch. I liked her. She showed up everywhere I played and took a front row seat. I was not her caliber of client, but she respected my talent, and we became good friends. We were going to meet for lunch on Sunset Boulevard at Scandia, directly across from her office.

As I turned north off Sunset in search of a parking space, I nearly ran over a man in the crosswalk. When I slowed, he leaned his head into my open passenger window, "Are you going up the hill? My car is parked at the top and you could save me a lot of trouble walking." All six-feet-two of Jon Voight barely fit in the front seat of my tiny Dodge Omni hatchback. When he got in his knees were in his nose. The trip was too short to even ask for an autograph.

A Song of Apology

One evening in spring of 1986, two women, draped in full-length silver and red fox coats, came in and sat at the bar of the Bel Age Hotel.

"Everyone knows you don't wear fur this late in the season," my fashion-forward friend Eleanor Rudolph said condescendingly.

"Depends on what business you're in," I quipped.

The women gave me a confirming glare. Thinking nothing of it, I returned to the piano. A few minutes later a chill filled the room as Adnan Khashoggi entered, surrounded by a cluster of sinister characters. The two women joined them in the Franco-Russian dining room. Shortly after, one of Khashoggi's Saudi henchmen approached the piano. I anticipated a generous tip but received quite the opposite.

"You have insulted Mr. Khashoggi," he snarled. "He wants you to play a song of apology."

I paused, flushed with confusion.

"Play it now!" he said, pounding his fist on the piano lid. My blood went cold. He rejoined the party. Fearing for my life, I quickly closed the piano and left.

I spent summer that year on the Costa del Sol of Spain. My friend Kate McAloon and I were invited to a party on a yacht in Puerto Banús harbor. I learned that we would be visiting *Nabila*, a massive vessel that belonged to none other than Adnan Khashoggi. I shuddered.

Because of its size, the colossal 281-foot ship had to be docked along the outer breakwater of the harbor. Elizabeth Taylor and George Hamilton were delivered by helicopter as we were arriving. Boarding the vessel, Kate pointed to the right of the gangway at what I assumed were mammoth sterling silver letters: N-A-B-I-L-A. She corrected me. "They're platinum." What else would one expect from the richest man in the world?

I'll Give You Forty Bucks

Coachella Valley Music and Arts Festival, more commonly known as Coachellafest, annually showcases popular and emerging musical artists. Snoop Dogg, Paul McCartney, and Madonna are among artists who have appeared at the desert's reincarnation of Woodstock. In my opinion, it's just a mass of typical twenty-something-year-old concertgoers getting drunk, disorderly, and arrested. During festival seasons, I performed at Amoré, a high-end nightclub and restaurant in neighboring La Quinta. One evening the manager came to the piano with a forty-dollar tip from a patron who requested that I "take a long break." I was perplexed, but agreed.

My regular listeners, Ray and Sheila, were in the audience, and made a special request for my return to the piano. "It will be a while," I told them. "The management asked me to take a long break."

"What's up with the long break?" Ray boldly addressed the

manager, Mark.

"Roger Waters is having dinner tonight and prefers that Jere not play."

Ray pulled a crisp one hundred-dollar bill from his pocket. "Who the fuck is Roger Waters?" He then turned, handed me the bill and said, "You know Sheila's favorite song."

I returned to the piano. I still don't know who the fuck Roger Waters is!

Just Follow the Circle

Tom Jones performed after Liberace at the MGM Grand in Las Vegas in 1983. Dale and I were invited to his show and seated with his dear mother, Freda, at a VIP table in King's Row. Following the concert, we went backstage and were introduced to Tom, who gave me the advice I believe he uses to this day.

"Throughout my life I go in a big circle, continually grabbing opportunities that come within my reach." As he said this, his hand arced, making a circle and randomly poking at the air within his reach. He has obviously maintained his own philosophy. He's in his seventies and still performing.

Flick Your Pick

I went to see Wynonna Judd, a truly captivating personality, at Caesar's Palace in Las Vegas. Her manager made our seating arrangements, and we were right underneath her nose at the lip of the stage. Wynonna came out and rocked the showroom. About three songs into the performance she came to the edge of the stage, winked, threw me a kiss, and flicked her guitar pick. The pink guitar pick landed directly on the table, right in front of me. I thought, *How the hell did she do that?!* I still have the guitar pick. I cherish that pick. I just wish I played the guitar.

Bewitched, Bothered, and Bewildered

At my apartment in West Hollywood, I had some *faaab*-ulous parties. One still haunts me. Four of the characters from the *Bewitched* television series showed up: Elizabeth Montgomery (Samantha Stephens) was twitching her nose at the buffet table while Dick Sargent (Darrin Stephens) looked on. Bernard Fox (Doctor Bombay) avoided Paul Lynde (Uncle Arthur) who held court in the living room. The typical group of friends who usually attended my parties was in awe of my guests that evening. I must admit, it was impressive … or should I say … bewitching?

Song on the Sand

Betty and Gene Barry came to enjoy my music while in the piano bar of Lyons English Grille in Palm Springs. I recognized Gene from his classic TV series *Burke's Law*. I was always impressed when they showed him at the beginning of the program being chauffeured in his Silver Rolls Royce Cloud through the streets of Beverly Hills.

On one occasion, while dining Gene put his fork down, came to the piano, and asked me to hit a chord in the key of F. He burst into a sentimental rendition of "Song on the Sand," his romantic number from the Broadway production of *La Cage Aux Folles*. The crowd was enchanted, and a pattern emerged. From then on, any time that I was at the piano and Gene Barry was present he would give me a wink, I would hit the key of F and he would break into "Song on the Sand." As time passed, Gene began to forget the lyrics and turned to me in anger mistakenly blaming me. "You're in the wrong key."

Later on, I received a call from Gene asking me to accompany him at a concert he was giving at the McCallum Theatre in Palm Desert. Although I was flattered, I turned down the opportunity after his wife Betty called pleading, "Don't do it." She feared that Gene would lose his concentration in the middle of the performance. "I'm trying to discourage him from doing the show."

And Betty was right. Gene insisted on performing at the ill-fated event. His memory failed midway, as before, and he left the stage. "The Song on the Sand" bit the proverbial dust.

This Is My Table

Popular showman Breck Wall arranged for me to see Kenny Kerr, famous female impersonator, at the Sahara Hotel in Las Vegas in 1982. I sat at a table with Joan Rivers, who was engaging and amusing. While leaving the showroom after the performance, I hugged her entourage to look like I belonged. As we moved along, she parted the waters—slot machines ceased to ring, dealers froze, and gamblers gawked and nudged their neighbors.

During my years with Liberace, Joan and I eventually became friends. Two things Joan always says when she sees me: "He stole my material" and "He let me sit at his table."

Happy Birthday, Screw You!

At a lush birthday party for a prominent local businessman in Venice Beach, California, celebrities munched and mingled as cameras flashed and everyone partied. As a giant cake was rolled out, I found my way to the grand piano in the middle of the room. Being not so shy, I sat down and began to bang out "Happy Birthday." The crowd caught on and joined in toward the end of the chorus. When I modulated keys and repeated the song, the guests crowded the piano. A woman on my right put her hand on my shoulder at the end of chorus and said, "Play it one more time." I turned, and there was Julie Andrews. On the third round, I felt a hand on my left shoulder and turned, there was Carole Burnett. The hired photographer was poised at the end of the piano. "Take a picture … *quick!*" I barked. The photographer scowled but snapped the shot.

I found her later on in the party, handed her my card, and requested a copy. "Oh, I'm so sorry," she said, voice dripping with sarcasm. "There wasn't any film in the camera."

I knew she was lying, and I was pissed.

Happy Birthday, and screw you!

Can You Take Out the Trash, Dear?

A guy picked me up in a bar in West Hollywood and invited me to his house for the night. Need I say more? The next morning I pieced together my way home. New to Los Angeles and unfamiliar with the Hollywood Hills, I just started walking. My only sense of direction was that I lived downhill, that way. As I strolled along I noticed a woman taking her trashcans out to the curb. I approached to ask if there was a good place for breakfast nearby. She was wearing a wide-brimmed garden hat. When she raised her head, I recognized Lily Tomlin.

Recently in Palm Springs I was standing in the queue at Walmart and noticed a familiar woman in a wide-brimmed garden hat. "Miss Tomlin?"

She turned, lowered her glasses and said, "Yeeeessss."

"I am sorry to hear about Momma Tomlin's passing."

"Do I know you?" she inquired.

"I know your brother Richard," I said. "I'm Jere Ring. You and I met years ago in the Hollywood Hills when you were taking your trash out."

She responded, "Was it anyone I knew?"

CHAPTER 4

Puttin' on da Dawg

The world is filled with dog lovers. I have petted pooches in all four corners of the planet. A common denominator that pampered pedigrees have is their eccentric, overly protective masters. Celebrity-owned dogs of notable backgrounds are no different from the neighbor's mutt. They all pant, drool, sniff butt, and occasionally snarl, snap, and bite. Join me as I introduce you to a hodgepodge of howling hounds and their avant-garde owners, and I'll let you determine which one is really … *Puttin' on da Dawg.*

Your Pillows Are Panting!

Before I was aware of who or what I was going to become, I dated a variety of young women. One of the determining factors was initial appearance—self-esteem is inevitably elevated when accompanied by an attractive person, of any sex. The snappy chicks from the Park-Tudor student body were most times already claimed, and the selection of girls that remained were common, lackluster, or mildly repellent, therefore dramatically narrowing my range of options. So to pique the interest of my prep-school chums, I would issue an invitation to a knockout babe from another high school.

The girlfriends I made at school were, as a rule, friends who happened to be girls. Two of my favorite female friends were the famous Ball twins, Julie and Janet. They were easy on the eyes, witty, amusingly audacious, and had little to no regard for the school's agenda and rules. The three of us were often called to the office of headmaster or mistress where theatrical lecturing fell on deaf teenage ears. The majority of the students at Park-Tudor were the products of wealthy families. The Ball twins birthright fell into the category of American Aristocracy. Granddaddy William Charles Ball co-founded Ball Brothers Glass Manufacturing Company, internationally known for manufacturing the ever-popular home canning jar.

With a twinkle in her eye, Julie once told me about the life-size oil painting of her entrepreneurial patriarchal ancestor that graced a prominent wall somewhere on the campus of Ball State University. The family had nobly placed an emblematic bronze plaque below the imposing portrait, proudly declaring that the notable work of art had been "Hung by the Balls."

William and his wife Agnes Ball lived grandly in a foreboding mansion in Golden Hill, an exclusive borough established in the early twentieth century near the city-center of Indianapolis. One evening as the girls and I set out on a typical Saturday night rampage, Julie suggested that we stop by the "manor" so that she could present me to her grandmother. I was both thrilled and daunted by the prospect of such an introduction.

We arrived at the house just as the last of the evening light vanished, giving an eerie edge to the scene. Upon our arrival, "Lurch," as Janet affectionately addressed him, responded to the ringing doorbell, swung the massive door open wide, and guided us through the entry to a spacious room filled with priceless antique furnishings, objects d'art, and paintings. A tremendous Persian rug graced the elaborately detailed hardwood floor. In the center of the room was a colossal sectional divan that squarely faced the broad, arched opening from the vestibule. Lurch announced our arrival from the foyer and disappeared down a long corridor.

Upon entering the room, I was so overwhelmed with elaborate décor that I failed to notice a petite woman, poised in a pale Chinese caftan at the center of the sectional. The colors of her generous silk dressing gown blended so very closely with multitudes of multihued pillows that surrounded her that she all but appeared as another throw puff.

Julie quietly spoke as we moved toward the center of the room. "Nana. I have someone I want you to meet."

The grand lady rose and balanced herself with a gold-crowned ebony walking stick, and slowly ascended from the sofa. She adjusted her gown, placed her walking stick a short distance in front of her right foot, and began to walk toward me. As she did, my eyes were fixed on her glowing smile. I started to introduce myself but was distracted by a wave of curious motion surrounding the tiny woman. The collection of pastel pillows began stirring and popping onto the floor. They hit the surface of the rug with tiny feet and advanced. As they came closer, tiny black eyes and wet noses appeared! Toy poodles. A dozen of them! Pallid tiny toy poodles. Unbeknownst to me, Agnes Ball owned a poodle farm. She constantly surrounded herself with these petite four-legged wonders, which she lovingly raised and then dyed in a variety of soft colors. By the flicker of amusement in her expression, it was apparent that Grandmother Ball had observed the gaze of astonishment on a host of other faces before mine.

"I am very pleased to meet you," she said quietly as she extended her hand. "I trust you like dogs."

I smiled and nodded. "I do, very much."

We enjoyed an aperitif and a nice conversation together. After some sniffing, sneezing, and an occasional lick, all of the pillows assumed their original spots on the divan, with their elegant master settled amongst her brood. We bid farewell and left the Mansion on Golden Hill.

Dog on the Run

The southern border of the Beverly Hills Flats was lined with a variety of beautiful gardens. I often walked the trail with my schnauzer Logan. As I was driving into Beverly Hills one day, I spotted an impressive St. Bernard trotting on the trail. He was alone and on the move. When I reached Rexford Drive, I made a sharp right and blocked the crosswalk. He slid to a stop. When I opened the door and walked around the front of the car, the dog stood erect, ears poised, and stared. I knelt and extended my hand, and his expression changed and he came directly to me. The St. Bernard's clean coat glistened and his fluffy fur was fragrant. This lovable guy was somebody's pampered pooch. I opened the back door to my Town Car, and, without hesitation, the dog jumped in. After slipping behind the wheel, I turned around and searched for a collar in his thick mane of fur. His dog tags had a phone number on them. I quickly located a pay phone, dialed the number, and reached a Latina woman who exclaimed, "Oh, we've been looking for him everywhere! Where is he? We come get him …"

I explained he was in the back of my car, filling the whole seat. She gave me an address in Bel Air and I headed for the hills.

When I arrived at the house, I pressed the bell button and the gates opened. I pulled up to the front entrance where a beaming Art Linkletter was waiting on the porch. I opened the car door and the happy hound rocketed out of the back. Mr. Linkletter asked how he could repay me. I answered with a request for an autographed picture. He signed it; I took it and left smiling.

Master of the Hounds

When I am in England, I like to visit the little village of Chackmore located at the foot of Stowe, the former country estate of the Duke of Buckingham. The centuries-old hunt club was one of the last of its sort, still managed by a master of the hounds, Mr. Dimbledy. One afternoon over a pint, he invited me to join him for the walking of the hounds. At 6:00 a.m. the following morning, I joined him and sixty-two tail-wagging, smiling beagles. He knew every one of them by name. As we began the five-mile trek, Dimbledy shared the history of Stowe.

The Duke of Buckingham sold his London residence to afford maintaining his country estate. In anticipation of the greatly coveted visit from Queen Victoria, the Duke enhanced the views from the path with decorative statuary, landscaping and fountains. As we strolled the path, we greeted people from the village and surrounding areas whom Dimbledy also knew by name.

"Hello, Lady Frothly … Beautiful day, Mr. Sher … Good Morning, Sir Elton!"

Many paces down the way, it struck me. The last man had looked familiar. I turned to Dimbledy and asked, "Was that Elton John?" Dimbledy boasted, "It was indeed!" I ran back to look for Sir Elton John, but he was gone. Disappointed, I returned to Mr. Dimbledy and the hounds.

A Guiding Light

On a ten-day Alaskan voyage there was a charter group of eighty-six visually impaired passengers, twenty-six brought their guide dogs along. Nearly all of the considerate canines were yellow labs or golden retrievers. They were a gregarious bunch! When the dogs were working they were focused and disciplined.

Three times a day the dogs were brought to the open deck amid ship where they were allowed playtime on the green low-pile Astro Turf. They were released with a command for play. It was delightful to see the twenty-six dogs jump, bark, roll, and wrestle. The guide dogs were brilliantly trained. When the order was given, they ceased to play and stood at attention. They would only speak when spoken to and even pooped on command.

The featured celebrity onboard was Roselle who led her master and thirty other people from the seventy-eighth floor of tower one of the World Trade Center on 9/11. With his hero-dog at his side, owner Michael Hingson shared many moving stories onstage during the cruise. Of the many voyages I have sailed, that was one of the most memorable.

You Bitches All Look Alike

Our black standard poodle, Jozelle, was a gift from some very generous fans. My partner Johnny and I drove to Northern California to pick her up from a breeder. Being one of eleven pups in the litter, they painted her tail bright green so that we would know she was ours. When she finally came of age at four months, we took Jozelle to the Palm Springs Dog Park. As we stood in proud admiration of our little girl I said, "This dog is growing legs like Susan Anton."

Johnny looked at me puzzled, "Who's Susan Anton?"

I sniggered and informed him, "Susan Anton is a famous tall, blonde singer and dancer." Pointing out a woman standing nearby I added, "That young lady looks like Susan Anton."

The woman overheard me, turned and said, "I am Susan Anton."

I threw up my hands, "You bitches all look alike!"

CHAPTER 5

Boys Will Be Girls

Don't be surprised if the attractive businesswoman who just closed escrow on your new home used to be on the high school football team with your son. The flawless creature behind the makeup counter may have been in your husband's Boy Scout troop. Karl, the new member of your Monday night football buddy bunch, was formerly named Kathy and married to your second cousin Troy over in Peoria, Illinois. Transgendered, but not hindered.

Ahhhhh … The marvels that evolve when technology and modern medicine convene with liberal lifestyle! I am very happy to introduce you to this intriguing array of fascinating people who account for some of my most-admired friends. You may very well make some "changes" in your own life when you discover why … *Boys Will Be Girls!*

I'll Be Back When I'm a Star!

I met Victoria Wilson James in a trendy hair salon at Lazarus Department Store on the north side of Indianapolis. She was a wild black girl, tall, slender and stylish. We wined and dined all over the city, danced in the discos, and ravaged the gay bars. She was heartbroken when I moved to California and followed me a few years later. When she arrived in Los Angeles she was different.

For our first reunion, we rendezvoused at the Old World restaurant on Wilshire Boulevard. She walked through the front door; eyes fixed on me, she sashayed her way over. She stopped at my table, kissed me on the cheek and purred, "Hey, baby." I was gobsmacked. We spent a delightful evening re-igniting our friendship. In a revealing conversation she shared that she "had everything done." Unbeknownst to me she was a boy when I met her way back in Indianapolis.

Victoria was hired as a counter manager, one of the flawless creatures, for Prescriptives cosmetics at Nordstrom. She started seeing a psychiatrist to help her adjust to her social transition. The doctor breached confidence and exposed her; Nordstrom fired her. She successfully sued the company for defamation of character and damages. Shortly thereafter, Victoria let me know that she was leaving for Europe.

She said, "I won't be back until I am a star."

Years later I received a call from a British talent manager who invited me to a concert at the Gibson (then, Universal) Amphitheatre in Hollywood. Victoria Wilson-James was the new lead singer for the popular group Soul II Soul. While in America she was featured on talk shows and made personal appearances. I visited her often at her homes in both London and Amsterdam. Backed by Sony, Miss V is now one of the top-recording artists in Europe and her star continues to rise and shine.

The Little Drummer Girl

Whenever Megan West was at my show I was happy to see her, and offer her the microphone. She had a scooby-doo scat technique that rivaled Ella Fitzgerald. Megan is also a brilliant musician. For many years she conducted her twenty-two-piece big band from the drums. She had her reassignment surgery at the Oregon Health Services University Hospital over two decades ago. "I have a stamp on it," she says, "'Made in the USA.'"

When I asked Megan who she was before the reassignment she replied, "I used to be Cassius Clay before, and I was transgendered so that I could become the punching bag." After Megan had her operation, she and her ex-wife became best friends. Megan has proudly spent the last decade in Las Vegas teaching music to special-ed children. No one in Vegas cared that she was a transgender.

Gypsy

James "Gypsy" Haake is eighty-one and "still above ground." His self-deprecating humor has brought him front-and-center stage in the world of female impersonators. I frequently sat in the packed house at his famous club La Cage Aux Folles in Los Angeles. The gangsters who owned the club embraced him. Gypsy is best known for his glittering gowns, flamboyant hats, and speaking in his deep baritone voice—one that's made cameo appearances in scores of movies and television shows. Gypsy is proud to let everyone know that he is a great-grandfather.

Transgendered But Not Hindered

Johnny and I stumbled off the elevator on the Ocean Princess. I said, "My gosh those people were weird." Johnny mildly observed, "They were sex changes." We later learned it to be true.

She to he and he to she and they were married. She (he) was married for twenty-six years with four children. He (she) had been married for twenty-four with three. They simultaneously divorced and married each other minutes before reassignment surgery. They were on board the ship to attend her (his) class reunion. She (he) was a graduate of the Naval Academy in Annapolis, Maryland with a degree in Naval architecture from MIT. The guys were really surprised to see him (her). Or was that her (him)?! He (she) was the CEO of a major national corporation. I never knew until I met her (him) and him (her) that there was a renowned international society for them. This may be confusing to you and me, but it certainly wasn't to them!

I Thought She Was a Guy

Lester Wilson had a crush on me. He was an Emmy-nominated choreographer, best known for his choreography in *Saturday Night Fever*. He entertained like he danced, with great panache. His close friends Diana Ross, Billy Crystal and Ann-Margaret frequented his soirées.

One night at a party at Lester Wilson's home, I noticed a short guy in a white T-shirt, overalls, and a baseball cap sitting cross-legged in the middle of a worshipful group. When he got up to leave I asked Lester who the young man was.

"You didn't recognize her?" Lester responded. "That was Madonna."

"I thought she was a guy," I replied.

"So does she," said Lester.

That's Why the Lady Is a Tran

When Lady April Ashley divorced Lord Rowallan, Parliament passed a law that transsexuals could not legally marry in England or the Commonwealth. She was the first sex change in England, having had her reassignment surgery in Casablanca, Morocco, in 1960. I met Lady Ashley in Los Angeles in the mid-1980s. She would to come to my parties in a ball gown, filling most of the room. Avery Van Arthur turned to her in the crowded living room of my apartment, "Lady Ashley, you look lovely but we need space!"

April was truly a lady, until she had too much to drink. Her long-concealed male characteristics surfaced and she would bark commands in every direction as if she were back in the palace: "Do you know who I am? I'm Lady Ashley!"

One of the most memorable days with Lady Ashley began with a morning of mimosas, and then we decided to go to the beach. It was cool, so she bundled up in a long silver fox coat, and I grabbed my full-length mink. On the way to the beach, dressed as we were, I came up with a better plan: "Instead, let's go to the Ritz Carlton in Laguna." And we changed direction.

On the way to the Ritz, still sufficiently sloshed from the mimosas, I had an even crazier idea to visit my friend serving time in an Orange County correctional facility. When we entered the jail, Lady April commented, "We look like the Duke and Duchess."

"Or the King and Queen, but we would have to fight over those titles," I quipped.

When we left she moaned, "Now I really do need a drink!" So off we went to the Ritz.

It was dark by the time we left the Ritz Carlton, and we were in much worse shape than when we started. I made a wrong turn somewhere along the way and we ended up in downtown Los Angeles. At a stop light a knife-wielding thug opened April's unlocked door and demanded that she get out of the car. "Well, allow me to get my purse," she parlayed. "I'm certain there's something in there that you want."

She opened her handbag and produced a Dillinger and shot him in the left foot.

She slammed the door and commanded, "Drive." What a lovely day that was!

Do Ask, Do Tell!

Christine Jorgensen was the first in the United States to have sex-reassignment surgery. They docked her dick in Copenhagen in 1951. She was an instant celebrity when she returned to the States. Christine used to hang out at The Main Street, a little Laguna Beach gay bar that I was playing in. Her good friends Marion Rhodes and Kay Dexter, wealthy lesbians, owned the club and maintained a beautiful home in Laguna. All three were joined at the hip, and I always imagined that there was more to the friendship than I viewed from the piano … A visual that I could certainly do without!

Ich Bin Froh, Dass Es Gegangen Ist

I met Marlene Parker at a Beverly Hills pool party. With boobs the size of basketballs, she was floating in the pool. I stood and stared at her and she lowered her sunglasses. She spoke with a thick German accent, "They keep me afloat, dahling." Marlene was the first sex change in Germany. Once a beautiful young man and a member of the German Olympic swim team, she became a beautiful woman. She was and still is the toast of Hollywood. Glamorously gowned she glows at galas, always making a grand entrance. When I saw her last, she shared something that she had never divulged before: "Ich bin froh, dass es gegangen ist!" which translated means, "I'm glad it's gone!"

What a Party!

My parties were good, really good, but this one was great. I invited April Ashley, Christine Jorgensen, and Marlene Parker, and they all came. My friend Gail Dauer, my favorite Beverly Hills Jewish transplant from New Jersey, stood in the middle of the room and squawked, "Jere! This is amazing! All three of them are here! You should sell tickets!"

CHAPTER 6

You're Only as Good as Your Last Party

The expression "Keeping up with the Joneses" is an underestimation in Beverly Hills Society. Tummy tucks, lifts, and peels are part of a normal agenda for both men and women. Cars, jewelry, oversized mansions are paramount to stay afloat in the A-list societal structure. An employee at Beverly Hills Loan once furtively shared with me that the wife of a renowned producer surreptitiously pawned suites of Harry Winston jewels on a monthly basis. She would return when she could coerce the bucks from her unsuspecting husband and return the jewels to the safe deposit box. As Carol Snow wrote, "Here today, gone to Maui!"

Take the star tour of some of the most expensive real estate in the world, and behind the gates of some of the imperious palaces you'll see are the biggest headaches in history. Social rivals set vindictive plans into motion between luncheons and spa visits. How many times can you get your picture in the society pages and can you really afford the price of putting it there? Wanna be royalty? No problem! Buy a title!

Find out who is and who ain't as we slog through the world of faux gentility where the motto is … *You're Only as Good as Your Last Party.*

Stick Around for the Jew Food

I met Bob and Beverly Cohen at a splashy Bel Air bash in the mid-'80s. She was blond and brassy. He was sensible and slightly portentous. In the wake of a conversation at the party, I was invited to walk through the job site of the new Beverly Hills Four Seasons Hotel with its owners, the Cohens. Bob wanted my opinion on where to place the piano within the configuration of the hotel's bar and lounge. While stepping over piles of sand, brick, and boards, I viewed the succession of unfinished rooms with a performer's eye and chose what I considered to be the most advantageous spot to place a gleaming grand. But my hopes of stepping behind the keyboard were soon dashed when Bob mentioned that they had already chosen the lucky guy who would be entertaining the chic clientele. The inimitable Dana Bronson assumed the much-coveted spot and has sustained a healthy relationship with the hotel since it's opening in 1987.

As I developed a friendship with the Cohens their collective and individual eccentricities became more apparent. Beverly was determined and focused and possessed a watertight ability to intimidate. Bob was subtly prevailing. He was a consummate master gardener. He personally supervised all that went on at both the hotel and the Newport Beach residence. His passion for gardening was parallel to his method of living. Everything had its place and required patience and nurturing. Attention to detail was most important. He was confidant that his garden and his investments would grow, and indeed they did. I often saw him at the Los Angeles Wholesale Flower Mart at Seventh and Wall Streets. He always gave a friendly nod and a sincere, but concise, salutation. He was the same in his office, pleasant but never enough to disrupt his focus. The only time I ever saw him unwind was over a glass of wine at a party or when he had his fingers in garden soil.

I went to the penthouse on one particular morning to pick up a check. Beverly said Bob was upstairs in the bedroom suite. When I reached the top of the stairs, he came into view, sitting in pajamas with his right foot precariously resting on the gilded edge of an ornate

Louis XV Boulle style desk. He was trimming his toenails. He looked up and said hello and nodded to a nearby envelope. He didn't lose his focus or offer up any form of apology. He continued arduously on with his chore.

The Cohens had an incredible expertise for entertaining. They ran after exotic themes that outdid the mostess of any hostess in Beverly Hills. Having access to the finest facilities was essential to their success. Since the hotel opened, the Cohens have maintained a luxury penthouse apartment on the top floor of the Four Seasons Hotel as well as the former waterfront home of John Wayne in Newport Beach. The Cohens allegedly paid $6.5 million for the property in 1988 and in 2002, much to the dismay of neighbors and avid Wayne fans, the house was demolished and a 12,500 square-foot home was built on the sight. I played for the lavish parties at the beach house, but one in particular stands out in my memory.

Beverly asked me to entertain for New Year's Eve. I carted my Kurzweil keyboard to Newport for the event. The waterfront patios were bedecked in gold and silver lamé and hundreds of votive candles twinkling into the night. The guests danced to my music until one o'clock, when the crowd began to disperse, leaving a small group of revelers. Knowing no bounds, Beverly decided that she wanted to take a harbor cruise on the P'zazz and commanded the captain to weigh anchor and set sail. I was enjoying a much-needed bathroom break, and when I returned to the patio, I was dumbfounded to see my new electric keyboard suspended from the yacht's starboard hoist, dangling over the water. Beverly had ordered a handful of the crew to heave it onto one of the upper decks of the ship. Once the pricey piano landed on its feet, I continued to warble as we sailed into the new day.

Meatballs to Go

Carol Lawrence is, was, and always will be, a fabulous cook and hostess. It's not surprising considering her stanch Italian heritage. Proof is in her cookbook *I Remember Pasta: A Celebration of Food, Family and Friends*. I was very pleased when I was invited to her renowned holiday parties in the early 1980s. Her friends and confrères were so numerous that she found it necessary to divide the guest list and allocate it among several nights during the month of December. Carol cooked up bountiful bowls of a variety of pasta: perfect spaghetti al dente, rigatoni, and manicotti, with savory meatballs and gravy. She lovingly prepared these substantial servings of food with the purpose that each of her guests would go home with a bag of culinary treasures.

I met Carol Lawrence in Big Bear, California, at a Christian Bible Retreat organized by the Bel Air Presbyterian Church back in 1980. Shortly after I arrived, drawing numbers from a hat assembled Bible-study pairs. I was pleased when Carol and I were linked. Upon meeting with her for the first time, I shared how as an awestruck kid, I had admired her dancing and singing in the audience of the Starlight Musicals theatre in Indianapolis. I also had to share my admiration for her striking husband, Robert Goulet—I was unaware that she and Bob had been separated for four years and were in the midst of a divorce. Carol was brilliantly composed as she discussed the issue with amazing reflection and self-confidence. I was going through some tempestuous challenges of my own and found her candor and concern to be extremely helpful. We developed a rapport over time. In the wake of the Bible Retreat, we saw one another at Sunday worship, and I attended parties at her Los Angeles home. She was also on the disastrous SS *Sitmar Fairwind*, and threatened to leave the ship while I was on board in 1982.

Though I have not seen Carol for many years, I recall the night of one of her festive holiday affairs that I was unable to attend. If you couldn't be there for the party, she would send the party to you! She prepared enough food to feed a family of four and had it couriered to my apartment. To this day, I'm still looking for the Chianti …

Look! There Are My Doors!

In the early 1970s, one of the more prominent residences of Beverly Hills was given a new look. And it wasn't a very popular one. Sheikh Mohammed Al Fassi (who's sister had married Prince Turki bin Abdul Aziz, brother of Saudi king, Fahd al Saud) moved into 9577 Sunset Boulevard and transformed the once magnificent thirty-eight-room mansion into a party palace. The pristine white stucco exterior was painted baby poop green. Important Romanesque statues that prominently lined the perimeter of the property were garishly embellished with flesh tones and accentuated private areas. It was a neighborhood embarrassment.

On January 1, 1980, the house on Sunset caught fire and was burned beyond repair. My friends, Gail and Roger Dauer, purchased the house in 1985 and invited 1,000 guests for a champagne demolition of what remained of the dismal structure. A few days before the annihilation bash, Gail phoned and asked if there was anything that I would like to have as a souvenir from the house before it was razed. I asked for the iconic gilded front doors. She generously granted my wish and within an hour, I organized a handful of muscle men and the doors were mine!

On January 1, 1980, the house on Sunset caught fire and was burned beyond repair. My friends, Gail and Roger Dauer, purchased the house in 1985 and invited 1,000 guests for a champagne demolition of what remained of the dismal structure. A few days before the annihilation bash, Gail phoned and asked if there was anything that I would like to have as a souvenir from the house before it was razed. I asked for the iconic gilded front doors. She generously granted my wish and within an hour, I organized a handful of muscle men and the doors were mine!

The doors are now prominently displayed in the entry of our Palm Springs home. The gilded side gleams while the opposite side still bears the charred scars of the fire that destroyed the mansion thirty-three years ago. One evening, while watching the movie *The Jerk*, with Steve Martin and Bernadette Peters, I was stunned to see the doors in a scene in the movie. Since that time, I have received a number of offers on the doors but they still remain, stately and standing tall, in our home. When I look at them and fondly recall that fun day at the Dauer's demolition bash.

Who Are You?

Oliver Stone recently hosted a party for his mother's ninety-second birthday. A bistro in La Quinta, California, was transformed into Studio 54, Jacqueline Stone's favorite New York City haunt from the 1970s. Ninety-two guests were assembled to commemorate her ninety-two years and each was given a nametag as they entered the club. Abba's "Dancing Queen" was blasting over the sound system as Jacqueline arrived. While everyone fawned over the birthday girl, I found a quiet Oliver Stone seated at the head table. Feeling unnoticed, I stood up in the middle of the room and belted out "Happy Birthday" a cappella. As the applause resounded, I took a seat next to Oliver. As we conversed, I could not resist asking the obvious: "Do you really think you need a name tag?"

CHAPTER 7

Too Much Is Never Enough!

There is an exceptionally small part of the world's population that takes pleasure in living a life of vast wealth. The standard of living for the members in this small society is mind-boggling. Princess Faridah of Brunei travels internationally with an entourage of eighty people and spends more money on shoes in one afternoon in Beverly Hills boutiques than most white-collar Americans earn in one year. Fully staffed homes in Bel Air, California, await the surprise arrival of part-time owners who rarely arrive. Mega yachts docked in the harbor Monte Carlo are traded and sold like baseball cards and many times never used. Private jets. Outrageous collections of exotic automobiles. How many homes can one person own?

Allow me to introduce you to some of the world's most ridiculously wealthy people as we travel into the whimsical world where ... *Too Much Is Never Enough!*

Bakker's Bought It All

I had the unique experience of sitting behind Jim and Tammy Faye Bakker at an antique auction. The peculiar couple pompously entered the auction house and Jim waved to the people as he walked down the aisle. Tammy Faye looked as though she had applied her makeup with a paint roller. Everything about her appearance was false from her eyelashes to her bogus bling.

Shortly after the couple took their seats in the front row, the bidding began. Selfish and indulgent, Jim raised his paddle and won the bid on almost every item. The crowd became heated, and buyers began to get up and walk out. Several hours later when the auction concluded Jim was the proud owner of a dazzling array of items. When I commented, "Wow. You really cleaned up!" he matter-of-factly replied, "Yes. Just more stuff to put in the warehouse."

The Arab Oil Sheik

It was a slow Tuesday evening at the Bel Age Hotel. The occupancy was low and the normally busy valet attendants were gathered in a conversational cluster at the entrance to the hotel. The lobby was quiet. The kids at the reception desk smiled and nodded as I passed. A maintenance man was on a ladder, replacing light bulbs in a lobby chandelier. Upon entering the piano lounge, I noticed a small man sitting at the far end of the bar. He turned and gave a nod as I opened the Steinway grand and completed my customary setup routine. I shared a hello and a how are you with Joe the bartender, and then went to the piano and began to play.

My only listener appeared to be a well-dressed Middle Easterner in a dark suit; tie neatly knotted and precisely placed under the nattily starched color of his white shirt. He was sipping champagne from a fluted glass with his right hand and twirling a box of Dunhill cigarettes with his left. *Twirl … tap … twirl … tap …* and then he suddenly stopped and removed a cigarette from the pack. With a sharp glance and a curious twinkle in his eye, he abruptly spun on the barstool and turned his back toward me. Was he writing something? Or perhaps, reading a bar menu? I segued from one tune to another and had just completed a Cole Porter medley when he spun around on the barstool, stood, and approached the piano. I smiled. He didn't. He stood quietly for a moment. Then he produced the Dunhill pack, opened it, and pulled one cigarette away from the rest and offered it to me.

I declined.

"I think you should take a cigarette."

I declined again.

He then placed the cigarette on the piano. "It's not a normal cigarette but I don't suggest that you light it." He then smiled and returned to his seat at the bar.

I left the cigarette there for a few songs. He would turn and shoot a fleeting glance my direction, and then turn back to his champagne. He finally made a full spin and studied me with arms folded across his chest. I surrendered to his doggedness and picked the cigarette up to examine it. I smelled it first. He smiled. It was odorless. I pressed it tightly between my thumb and forefinger. It seemed to be a bit too firm for a real cigarette. Was it chocolate? I pinched the filter and hesitantly looked at the opposite end. It wasn't tobacco but rather a note of some sort, tightly wound and precisely fitted inside of the delicate white wrap of paper. I was able to grip an edge of the curious stuffing between two fingernails and carefully began to extract the contents. As I did so, I circumspectly studied my observer and noticed a sparkle in his eye and a nascent smile on his lips. I successfully pulled the scroll from it's housing to discover that it was a one hundred dollar bill!

The element of surprise on my face delighted my curious onlooker. He began to laugh profusely. He bounced from his perch at the bar and vigorously came to the piano with his hand extended. "I am Omar," he said between unintentional laughter. "I was afraid that you would light the cigarette and then be very sorry you did," he conveyed with a very thick Arab dialect. "Enjoy!" he exclaimed and then returned to his seat at the bar and disregarded me the rest of the night.

The next evening, Omar was once again seated in the same location at the bar. He approached me at the piano and yet again, offered me a Dunhill cigarette. I most kindly obliged his offer. This nightly pattern repeated itself for almost a month during which time his reticence to communicate and relative timidity kept me at a controlled distance. And then, on a bustling Friday night, the silence was broken.

A very close friend of mine stopped in for a drink and a hello at the end of a busy day. Marilyn Watson was a realtor with Celebrity Properties in Beverly Hills. She was a tall, strikingly handsome woman with a background in beauty pageants that included a Miss America first runner-up title. She had been a big band singer and often joined me at the piano for a vocal number or two. On this particular night, while sharing a pleasant rendition of "When I Fall In Love," she unknowingly captivated Omar's attention. As a result, he demanded to meet her. I carried out his request. Shortly after introducing the two, Omar made an unforeseen proposal.

During the month of silence, the urge to privately investigate this man was unavoidable. I had questioned staff members and carefully queried management. In doing so, I discovered that he was an absurdly wealthy thirty-six-year-old Arab oil sheik. He was very discretely traveling with his wife and three children. The family was occupying one of the larger suites on an upper floor of the hotel while he simultaneously made use of a lesser accommodation on a lower level. A pied-à-terre, if you will. My little Arab cigarette vendor was quite the womanizer. A private chef and several servants and chauffeurs accompanied the family. They also brought with them unparalleled food stuffs as well as a private selection of wines, champagnes, and caviar. I never met the wife or saw the children. Such wealthy Arab men characteristically control their families with interminable dominance and undeniable authority. Omar was always by himself unless he was accompanying the family from hotel room door to limousine in the valet parking, a tactic that was carried out in swift silence. I also learned a great deal more about my new friend on this most revelatory evening.

Omar posed an unusual request that unabashedly revealed a romantic inclination. He had a propensity for mature women. Marilyn was in her late fifties, making her at least twenty years his senior. His request of me to negotiate a meeting with her turned into a fervent plea. I told him that she was a lady and would not be keen on going to his private lair. He gulped champagne as the evening progressed and became noticeably intoxicated as his pursuit intensified. In one last desperate plea, he came to the piano, removed his wallet from the breast pocket of his suit coat and emptied the contents into my tip jar. As the copious bills scattered on the top of the piano, he demanded, "Make it happen!" and returned to his seat at the bar. I finished playing a song and casually sauntered over to pick up the assortment of twenties, fifties, and hundreds that lay on both the piano lid and the floor. I acknowledged a handful of patrons with a smile and a wink and made my way over to speak to Marilyn. Following a whispered conversation, she grudgingly agreed to go along with my proposal. My suggestion was to make arrangements with both parties to meet at the Jacuzzi on the rooftop of the hotel at midnight. I discretely revealed the plan with Omar and it was confirmed. Marilyn made her exit, winking and softly squeezing Omar's arm as she left the lounge. She and I both knew that she had no intention whatsoever of carrying out her end of the deal.

Around 11:30, Omar stumbled out of the lounge and headed for his midnight rendezvous. He passed by the piano and grumbled a declaration of gratitude. I wished him well and told him to have a pleasant time. When I left the piano at 1:30 hours later, I went to the rooftop. Steam was rising into the starlit sky from the bubbling Jacuzzi but there was no one about. I said a quiet prayer that my little Arab friend would not hurt me and then went home to my own snug bed.

The following night, I arrived at the hotel lounge to find Omar perched in his designated bar stool, sipping his private reserve champagne and enjoying his contemptibly costly caviar. He immediately donned a hangdog expression when he saw me. He sprang from his roost and came to me. "I am so sorry" he exclaimed. "I went to my room and fell asleep last night," he said in desperation. "I hope your friend is not upset with me!"

"She showed at midnight and was terribly disappointed but said that perhaps, another time would work out better." Omar quickly churned out, "Maybe tonight?"

I improvised. "Marilyn left town today for Santa Barbara for a week."

With a look of total dejection, Omar told me that he was leaving on Monday to go home. I was the despondent character at that point. Strangely enough, I had developed a fondness for a particular brand of Dunhill cigarettes during the past month.

The piano lounge seemed improbably quiet when I returned the following Tuesday. The absence of my new Arab friend had left an inexplicable void in my life. I truly missed him coming to the piano, sporting his little sinister smile and offering me a Dunhill. Oh, and for the record, my matchmaking skills paid off quite nicely. He was carrying $3,720 in his wallet. I gave up smoking and pimping on that fateful night … The night that Omar left town!

Money Can Buy Everything

My initial voyage on the *QE2* was a painful experience. I took a late afternoon flight from Los Angeles, arriving too late to do anything but check-in to the Hilton Midtown and put my head on a pillow. I awakened the following morning to a bright sunny day of adventure and set out to conquer Manhattan. By the time I boarded the classic vessel late in the afternoon, I was exhausted. My plan was to take an exhilarating sail away from the New York Harbor, have a relaxed meal, and go to sleep. When I eventually located my cabin in the bowels of the vessel, my well-organized plan disintegrated. A hand scribbled note that read, "Mr. Ring … Six o'clock rehearsal, eight o'clock show," was taped to the cabin door. I was stunned! There was hardly even enough time to let the wrinkles hang out of my rhinestone-studded tails! I tore my suitcase open and began to organize my band charts on the floor of the cabin only to watch them curl and prune on the wet carpet that was saturated from a leak in a bathroom wall. I put my parts together as best I could and arrived at the cavernous showroom ten minutes late to find a less-than enthusiastic group of maudlin musicians.

Following a pitiable rehearsal, I took a stroll around the promenade deck and made my entrance. In the midst of my halfhearted performance, I made a poor decision to announce the presence of a rat that I unfortunately spotted in the middle aisle of the showroom. Not a small rat. A large, fat, long-tailed rat! Three-fourths of the anemic audience made a swift exit. Feeling nothing short of defeated, I completed the performance, took my bows to the three remaining members of my audience and lumbered back to my cabin.

The next morning, I was apprehensive to so much as leave my cabin for fear of being subjected to vicious ridicule for my meager showmanship. When I opened my cabin door, a very attractive young English couple in the corridor bubbled with compliments and invited me to join them for breakfast. Little did I know that a momentous friendship was about to be shaped over eggs and bacon.

Gary and Suzanne Edwards were the then-current grand ballroom dance champions in the UK. They were equally eloquent in conversation as they were exquisite on the dance floor. They were regulars on the ship and gave me the skinny on all the goings-on. The shortcomings of the ship far outweighed the good stuff. The carpets were worn and upholstery frayed. The ship smelled of mold and mildew and the occasional waft of a toilet in close proximity was overpowering. Gary and Suzanne said that the English captain and crew were pompous and arrogant. Peter Longley, the cruise director, was contrived and condescending. I could sense that he was more in touch with himself than he was his staff. I knew that I would never be invited back so I decided to make the best of what could have been an otherwise appalling experience.

The five-night voyage made three stops: Halifax, Nova Scotia; Newport, Rhode Island; and Boston. Gary, Suzanne, and I were joined at the hip and toured each of the ports with adolescent enthusiasm. Following their spectacular ballroom extravaganza on the final night of the voyage, we took a late-night stroll on the promenade deck and experienced something that has since besieged me. While standing at the rail on the starboard aft, we heard the sound of breaking glass. We leaned over the rail to see large black plastic bags, stuffed with trash being tossed from ship to sea. To this day, I regret not reporting that incident to maritime officials. At the time, I suppose I was in fear of the ramifications of making accusations. Now I think, what the hell, they had no intentions of inviting me back as it was. I could have caused some chaos with that bunch of louses! To this day I wish them sleep-less nights filled with shark-infested dreams!

The following year, Holland America contracted me to sail from Acapulco to Lima, Peru, on the SS *Rotterdam*. Various members of her crew knew her as the "Sea Witch." She was the last great Dutch "ship of state" and catered to a select group of well-seasoned travelers who affectionately referred to her as the "Grand Dame." She was retired in the fall of 2000 following a career of forty years as one of the most successful passenger ships of all time. She was exquisite. Rich wood and brass appointments enhanced the classic styling of the last of the great steam ships. The ten-day voyage was made all the more enjoyable because of someone special that I invited to travel as my guest … my mom! Shortly after we embarked the ship, there was a knock at the cabin door. I opened it to discover my best ballroom buds; Gary and Suzanne from the *QE2* cruise from hell. With the addition of Mama, we became an inseparable foursome and solidified a superb alliance.

In 1992, I was invited to join the inaugural voyage of the SSC *Radisson Diamond* out of Rauma, Finland. The inaugural christening celebration was held on the Thames River next to the famed Tower Bridge of London. I invited Gary and Suzanne to the festivities as they had since departed ships and were living in London. It was marvelous to be with them again and visit their home and meet the parents of my new British chums.

A couple of years zipped by and one afternoon, I received a phone call in Los Angeles from Suzanne. To my great surprise, they were in town and wanted very much to see me. Her voice maintained mystery and her typical sparkling character was suppressed. She apologized and said she would explain upon meeting. Within the hour, they both arrived in an ominous chauffeur-driven black limousine. Once inside my apartment, they both bounced with enthusiasm, simultaneously chattering away in an attempt to explain the recent advent of activities in their life. Somewhere in the frantic dialogue I was only able to retain something about the Sultan of Brunei, a royal princess, and a shitload of money. Before I knew it, they whisked me out the door and into the limo we went. I was instructed to say nothing about our conversation while inside the car. "Well, how have you been?" and "Oh, fine … and you?" all the way to the Beverly Hilton where we made our way to a massive suite on an upper floor where I was introduced to Princess of Brunei. Princess Faridah was the third wife of Prince Jefri aka His Royal Highness Pengiran Digadong Sahib Mal Pengiran Muda Jefri Bolkiah ibni Al-Marhum Sultan Haji Omar Ali Saifuddien Sa'adul Khairi Waddien. The country of Brunei was unremarkable until the largest single deposit of oil in the world was discovered in the early twentieth century. That's when the self-appointed royal family infiltrated the Western world and began buying pricey real estate all over the globe.

Princess Faridah added me to the entourage of eighty people who accompanied her when she traveled. I was appointed as the court jester. Whenever I made her laugh I was rewarded with fistfuls of cash. After finishing a concert at the Royal York Hotel in Toronto, one of her henchmen handed me an envelope and told me to count it. I went into the men's room, locked myself in a stall and sat down to tally out $10,000. The Princess could afford everything, including me!

The Gefilte Fishpond

During the pinnacle period of my years in Los Angeles, two of my favorite characters were Gail and Roger Dauer, an enormously wealthy young couple who had moved from Miami Beach to Beverly Hills in the early '80s.

Roger fancied himself as a developer and successfully lived up to his reputation by erecting a handful of massive spec houses on Benedict Canyon. Gail, Roger, and their two daughters, Michele and Jennifer, lived in one of the homes for approximately one year until they moved into their more permanent residence, a 12,324 square-foot mansion at the corner of Foothill Road and Sunset Boulevard in Beverly Hills.

The mansion boasted six bedrooms and twelve bathrooms and a full-sized racquetball court, located at the rear of the property, which underwent several transformations throughout the years. As none of the family members were even the least bit athletically inclined, the court was rarely used. The most popular sport in Beverly Hills that Gail had mastered was … Shopping.

Because her ever-changing, ever-expanding wardrobe was beyond comprehension, she decided to reawaken the lonely volley court by transforming it into her personal clothes closet. Due to its high ceilings, she was able to install an electric conveyor system as one might find in large dry cleaners. The simple push of a button conveniently summoned her choice of attire du jour from somewhere in the vast two-story space. Should she find it necessary to view the collection as a whole, the former observation window from the game room loft served a new purpose as well.

But alas, Gail grew weary of her larger than life itself walk-in closet and began donating bits of her wardrobe to auctions for worthwhile Beverly Hills charity functions. After all, it was the "thing" to do among society dames. Their names went in print, and they were offered unsparing kudos for their benevolent objectives. (And anyone who knows anything about anything must be aware that an outstanding $30,000 couture garment can only be worn once. Then it must be discarded! God forbid that one should suffer the humiliation of being seen wearing the same garment a second time!)

The mega-closet was converted into a ballroom. Renowned international interior designer Roy Sklarin was commissioned to complete the transformation. The finished product was truly dazzling. Much of the room was carpeted, but a portion of the relatively unscathed wooden planks of the sports floor were left exposed for dancing. A faux stonewall with cascading plants was erected on the perimeter, giving the illusion that one was in an outside courtyard. Above the "stone wall" sat a hand-painted three-dimensional mural of the Hollywood Hills, which reached, to the high ceiling, which was covered with twinkling lights, emulating a starlit sky. Gail called upon me to locate a glossy grand piano for the stage. I obliged and was asked to perform for "opening night" to which everyone from Esther Williams to Joan Collins was invited to share in the festivities. Through the years, I have attended many over-the-top soirées at Dauer Manor.

Just recently, I received a call from Gail informing me that they sold the house to a couple who just happened to be strolling by the house and inquired about a tiny for sale sign that had been unassumingly placed near the street. On May 5, 2009, Shirin Farzadmehr and Youram Nassir paid $7.5 million in cash for the house, and the Dauers moved on in life. They have begun construction on their new home just up the way in Beverly Hills. Talk about movin' on up! Their new bungalow will be 22,600 square feet with eleven bedrooms and fifteen bathrooms. I can't wait to go to that opening night bash!

CHAPTER 8

Fag Hags

We are the best dancers, best dressed, well traveled, meticulously groomed, successful, interesting, entertaining, and attractive. We open doors, pull out chairs, and tell women when they have lipstick on their teeth. We are their hairdressers, decorators, and fashion coordinators. We make them the beautiful creatures that they are. We are better than girlfriends because we don't compete, but rather compliment.

Many times, these elegant dames move through their lives with nothing but gay men. It is a convenient arrangement for all. The old crows reel in the attention and constant fussing. They find companionship and their husbands are freed from their nagging. The token gay toy boy lives a vicarious lifestyle through that of his matriarchal mentor. These ubiquitous relationships are found in all neighborhoods. Meet the ladies who lunch as well as the chubby high school outcasts as we meander through the unique world of ... *Fag Hags*.

The Bag Lady

To most people, Eleanor Rudolph came off as a bitch. She boldly strode through life with an attitude. She knew what she liked and could afford to have it her way. She enjoyed shocking people with her blatant comments. "I don't have any women friends!" she would exclaim to a total stranger at a cocktail party. "Women are cesspools! I have a few select friends and they are all gay men," she would proudly announce as she would put her arm through mine and smile endearingly. "Men are pigs! Trust me, after three husbands, I should know!"

Eleanor's grandfather was one of the founders of the city of Oshkosh, Wisconsin. I referred to her as The Bag Lady when I discovered that she was the heiress to the Oshkosh Luggage fortune. She playfully embraced the title. Her silver streaked black hair was always worn in a shoulder-length Lauren Bacall style. She liked knee length a-line skirts because they showed off her terrific legs and well-turned ankles. Upon introducing her to my brother he said, "If my wife had legs like yours, I would have six kids instead of two." She loved it!

My then partner, Dale Brunner, and I were Eleanor's best buddies. She sometimes invited Baron Herbert Hischmoeller and his partner, Mark Nixon for dinner. She loved to conspicuously arrive at posh affairs in Matthew West's black Jeep Wrangler. Franz and Dieter were gay brothers. They were fine gentlemen and made a handsome presentation at a dinner party. Eleanor became annoyed with a gushing maitre d' at La Chaumiere one evening. The fawning ceased when Eleanor announced, "If you come over here to kiss my hand one more time, I'm going to spread my legs!"

Eleanor Rudolph was as eccentric as she was entertaining. She adored Finlandia vodka and claimed that any other brand made her deathly ill. She always carried a flask of the stuff in her handbag for emergencies. We escorted Eleanor to a funeral for a friend. At the reception, she asked a server for a glass of ice. When it arrived, she glanced around the room and quietly filled it to the brim from a fifth of vodka that she had stashed in her handbag. She shrugged her shoulders. "I was in a hurry and couldn't find my flask." She took a long drink and said, "You know, I have a bad left foot but if I have enough vodka, I don't even know I have a foot."

Eleanor passed away in her 91st year. I don't know if it was the vodka or that bad left foot that done her in. She left her entire fortune to Dale. Maybe he knows!

Sugar Mama

It was the day before Thanksgiving in 1988. Teena Watson and I had flown to New York City for the weekend and checked into a large two-bedroom suite at the Pierre Hotel. I had not been to New York since I made a day trip from Yonkers on the train many years prior. That time, I ate hot dogs in the street, visited the Statue of Liberty and viewed the city from atop the Empire State Building. This time, I flew first class from Los Angeles and rode in a limousine to the hotel. This was a new adventure. It seemed odd to me. *Why would a wealthy older woman want to take a young man on a trip to New York? A woman I barely knew!*

When we settled into the suite on the afternoon of the first day, Teena handed me a Platinum American Express Card and sent me off to Bergdorf Goodman buy some new clothes. It was quite obvious that my blue blazer, khaki pants, and penny loafers were not to her liking. She phoned ahead and spoke to a salesperson, issuing specific instructions as to what she wanted me to have. I returned hours later with a Giorgio Armani pinstriped dark suit, Oleg Cassini tie, and Ferragamo shoes. I was confused. She was pleased. That evening, we had dinner at the Palm Court at the Plaza Hotel. We feasted on tartare of smoked salmon, wild mushroom risotto, and bananas Foster while she discussed some of her whims and expectations of me during our weekend getaway. The rest of the night went smoothly. We took a nightcap in the Café Pierre and retired somewhat early.

The next morning, I carried out my initial assignment for the order of the day: I was to fill a stemmed glass with champagne, add two ice cubes, then stealthily enter her bedroom and quietly place it on the bedside table. Teena's eyes were normally covered with a silk sleep mask as she slumbered. Once the pertinent pick-me-up was in place, I would tiptoe out of the bedroom and pull the door, leaving it slightly ajar. I recall smiling when I heard the sound of the tinkling of the cubes in the crystal flute as she picked up the glass to take her first motivating sip of the day … in the dark. She seemed to have an innate honing device for that glass. Once she rose from the bed, the glass of champagne never left her proximity for the morning. When room service arrived, we both sat at the rolling spread. She teasingly enlightened me that by adding a splash of cranberry juice to the bubbly libation, its nutritional value was mysteriously enhanced, hence justifying it as an appropriate beverage to accompany breakfast. And by continuously adding ice cubes throughout the day, she nursed the glass until five o'clock, at which time she made the transition to Scotch. The cocktail hour was when the dark clouds rolled in. That's when I discovered that she was an alcoholic. A bad one!

Teena and I traveled the world together for a number of years. We crossed the Atlantic Ocean on the *QE2* and returned on the Concord. We barged and ballooned the Rhône Valley in France and tasted wine in Brussels. We alternated between the Pierre Hotel in New York and the Breakers in Palm Beach for Thanksgiving, spent Christmas at the Grand Hotel Wien in Vienna and enjoyed Easter at the Halekulani Hotel in Honolulu. The Paris Ritz, the Ritz in London, the Hotel Cipriani in Venice and the Quisisana Hotel in Capri were regular haunts. We dined at La Tour d'Argent in Paris, Le Louis XV in Monte Carlo, and 1 Launceston Place in London. Teena thrived on researching fine dining and hotels around the world and planning exotic travels. I became her traveling companion, her confidant, and eventually, her bedfellow.

Teena was a relatively private individual. She was a classy dame. From what I could determine, she was not "to the manor born"; however, her mother's choice for a second marriage vaulted them into an affluent lifestyle thus enhancing their mark in society. Mr. Joyce was a prominent New York businessman. His wealth and influence landed young Teena, her elder sister and their mother in a Park Avenue apartment. They also had a country home in East Hampton and a notable residence in Palm Beach. After a decade of living on the East Coast, the family journeyed west, and moved into an "above Sunset Boulevard" mansion in Beverly Hills. They established memberships at the important private clubs and carved a niche for themselves in West Coast society.

Teena was a beautiful woman. She moved with style and grace. The generous jet-black hair of her youth was taken to platinum blond in her later years. She had porcelain skin and was always dressed with a sophisticated flair. She had aged with grace and had a sex appeal in particular arenas; she was also a temptress and always on the prowl for a man. Be it for a dance, a drink, a conversation and "whatever may happen" at the end of an evening. If asked how many times she had been married, her standard response was "Enough!" She was guarded about the subject but I calculated eight husbands from information gleaned in rare discussions on the subject. In between sips of Scotch during a particularly chatty cocktail hour at the California Yacht Club one evening, she revealed some luscious details. Paul Watson, her alleged first, was a horn player with the Freddy Martin Big Band. She claimed to have loved him dearly and kept his name. He stepped in front of a city bus. She spoke cautiously of a "black baseball player" who broke her arm. She did not confess to having been married to him; however, her subtle prejudicial inclinations suggested that memories of the incident lurked in the shadows of the past. Another unnamed husband met a tragic end when he was accidentally shot during a foxhunt on a private estate. She endured a six-month marriage to a Spaniard. Apparently, his inability to speak English posed some justifiably insurmountable challenges.

Over a decade, my alliance with Teena became one of immense trust and devotion. We had one intensely intimate night in Paris. From that point forward, I was made very aware that she wanted more from me than I was able and willing to offer. When I moved to Palm Springs, our bond began to diminish. I continued to make frequent trips to Los Angeles to visit her but our lives moved in different directions. I was sailing on the Coral Princess in Alaska when I received a call from her niece telling me that Teena had passed away. I spent that solemn sleepless night, wrapped in a blanket on the open deck under the stars.

The Boys Still Love Her!

For a short while in Palm Springs I was singing exclusively in gay bars. Concurrently I had a biweekly column in a local gay rag. Mona introduced herself to me at the piano at the Wild Goose and joined me in a song. We had an instant rapport. Within the week we became a dynamic duo. Mona Caywood and I moved on to The New Racquet Club. Toucan's became the trendiest club in town when Mona and I moved in.

Mona's popularity soared, and I gradually became her accompanist. For me, it was time for a change … so I grabbed Johnny and whisked him off for world travel on the high seas. Mona continues to flourish with the gay gigs and is recognized as the desert's Queen of Queens.

Why Did God Make Gay Men?

Why do girls love gay guys? Because we're fabulous, darling, and we adore our girlfriends! We have massive movie collections and love to watch chick flicks … over and over. We have current issues of *Architectural Digest, GQ, Gourmet, Travel and Leisure,* and *Men's Fitness* on our coffee tables. Our CD collections feature Madonna's *Immaculate Collection*, Bette Midler's *The Divine Miss M*, Judy Garland's *Judy at*

Carnegie Hall, and Patsy Cline's *12 Greatest Hits*, and everything by Lady Gaga, and we cry when we listen to them. If Michelangelo had been straight, the Sistine Chapel would have been wallpapered. Sigmund Freud's lover Wilhelm Fliess said "Freudian Slip" was inspired by either a lady's undergarment or a mishap in the shower. God created gay men … so that fat girl's would have somebody to dance with!

Being fitted for one of Liberace's costumes from the vault for the opening of the museum.

I was the first performer to wear one of Liberace's costumes in public.

Seated at the legendary Chopin piano.

With Dora Liberace.

Mom and me in a rare photo with the two brothers, George and Lee.

Ray Arnett on his 96th birthday.

South Korea.

A party in Fez, Morocco, hosted by King Hassan II.

Filming television special in Sydney, Australia.

Rastafarian photographer in Jamaica.

Digby goes overboard.

Visiting children in Malaysia.

Proposing on the Rock of Gibraltar.

With Johnny in Vietnam.

In the cockpit of the
Concord at 60,000 ft.

Mom and Dad in Naples, Italy.

Snorkel Johnny in Acapulco.

Dick Sherman, Disney composer, and his family on the MS Westerdam.

The Grand Bazaar in Istanbul.

At the Acropolis.

ROYAL PRINCESS

DUBLIN
EIRE
MAY 15, 1995

Having fun with flashcards on the Regal Princess.

GO AWAY

STICK IT IN YOUR EAR

SHOW ME THE MONEY

PUTZ

TAKE OFF YOUR CLOTHES

Lounging in the Bahamas.

Man overboard.

Mom and Dad on the
SSC Radisson Diamond.

Too much tequila.

Bathing beauty on the high seas.

Grace Robbins
in Marbella, Spain.

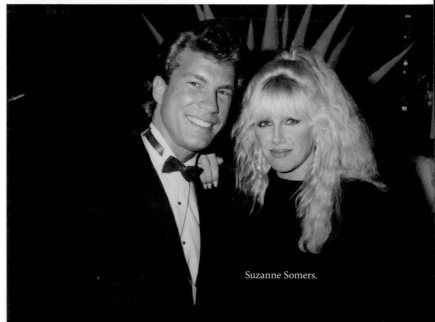

Suzanne Somers.

Eartha Kitt on
the Vista Fjord.

Kaye Ballard.

Michael Feinstein
at one of my
Hollywood parties.

Ricardo Montalbán.

Marty Allen on the Grand Princess.

Mom with Willard Scott.

Tom Jones and Dale Brunner in Las Vegas.

Ruta Lee and Toni Holt.

The Master of The Hounds at Stowe, England.

Guide Dogs lounging on the Regal Princess.

Salty and Roselle, hero guide dogs from 9/11.

My friend, Cindy Mills, with my favorite schnauzer, Logan.

Juno, my first dog in Indiana.

With Tag, one of Liberace's favorite dogs.

Libby, Linus, Molly, Tinker and Jay Jay.

Casey, the Wonder Dog.

With Supermodels Laura Costin and Jojo Juan.

Victoria Wilson James from her latest release, THE RAPTURE.
Photography: Cim August

The she-he, he-she
couple on the
Ocean Princess.
Transgendered but
not hindered.

Gypsy.

James "Gypsy" Haake.

Lady April Ashley.

Danny La Rue and
Lee Watson at the
Winter Gardens in
Blackpool, England.

Bob Hoven, tallest drag queen
in Palm Springs. 7'4" in hat and heels.

Marlene Parker, first and most glamorous 'change' in Germany.

Betty and Gene Barry.

Michael Feinstein
and Stan Freeman.

Jackie-Lee Houston,
the "Perle Mesta" of
the Desert.

Carol Lawrence.

Buddy Hackett, Sherry Sexton, Jan Murray, Donna Reed and friends at Chasen's.

Smartly dressed officers at a shipboard crew party.

With Teena "Sugar Mama" Watson
and her previous boy toy.

Jere and Eleanor Rudolph.

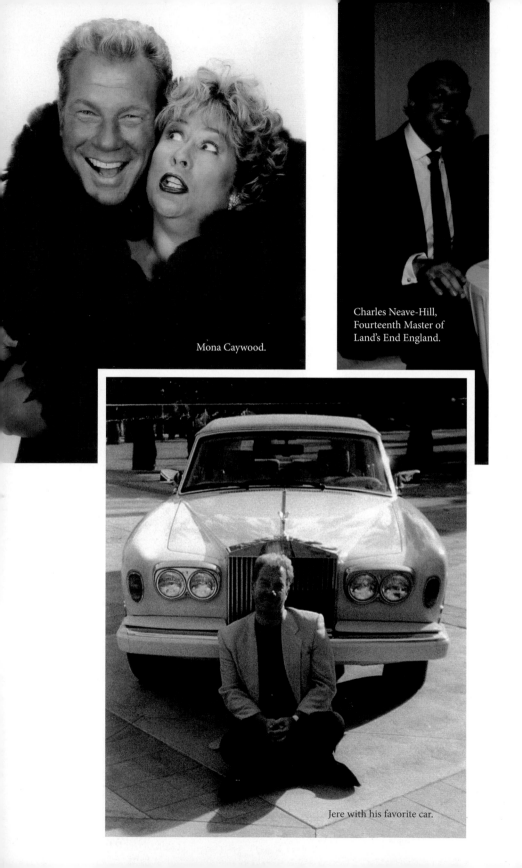

Mona Caywood.

Charles Neave-Hill,
Fourteenth Master of
Land's End England.

Jere with his favorite car.

With Aunt Thelma.

Aunt Thelma at the piano.

Driving Mrs. Daniel's
1961 Cloud Rolls Royce.

Robertine Buchanan
(Mrs. Daniels) in 1914.

Eleanor (Mrs. Rudy) Vallée.

Mr. And Mrs. Joseph Daniels in Vienna.

Kate McAloon, owner of the "Spirit of Ecstasy" in Puerto Banus, Spain.

Dame Shirley Bassey at the Red and Black Ball.

On a Hollywood set with Rudy Vallée,
Suzanna Foster and Skip. E. Lowe.

Boarding the Regal Princess with
Naomia Jean "Andraya" Sweet.

Johnny with Double D, Paula and Peaches at the Arctic Bar in Ketchikan, Alaska.

Eugene, no longer homeless and loving life on the Big Island.

Hermione Baddeley.

Tammy Wynette (falling out of her dress).

Deroy Green (Belafonte impersonator).

Debbie Reynolds.

Robin Leach on the
SSC Radisson Diamond.

Mr. Blackwell and Beryl Davis.

Patti LaBelle at my Gangie's 84th birthday party.

Shirley MacLaine and Mom at Tony Charmoli's Holiday party.

Off to the opera with
Ginger Rogers.

With Oliver Stone.

Jack Carter singing
at his own wedding.

Crossing my legs
with Phyllis Diller.

HRH Princess
Faridah of Brunei.

Dr. Elsa Colby Morley
in Beverly Hills.

Ruta Lee.

Sammy Davis Jr.
at Harrah's, Reno.

Mom and Carol Hinkley.

Bob and Cindy Mills, my biggest fans.

Entertaining Gangie on
Christmas day with Mom
and my nephews.

Mom and Dad.

Liberace

PRESENTS

JERE RING

Nightly in the Piano Lounge

Tivoli Gardens Restaurant
1775 East Tropicana
Las Vegas, Nevada
In the Liberace Plaza

THE
ROSE
TATTOO

665 North Robertson Boulevard, Los Angeles, California 90069 (213) 854-4455

PRESENTS

Jere Ring

S.S. AZURE SEAS
WESTERN CRUISE LINES
PRESENTS

JERE RING

APRIL 29 — MAY 27

CHAPTER 9

Home, James!

My first visit to Beverly Hills was brilliant. I was twenty and easily impressed with profligacy of wealth. I strolled Rodeo Drive with colossal arrogance, feebly attempting to mask the naiveté of my Hoosier roots. Priceless jewels glimmered in the windows of Harry Winston, Cartier, and Van Cleef & Arpels. Stunning fashions lured me to displays in Gucci, Giorgio Armani, and Battaglia boutiques. The extravagant city was indeed extraordinary but one particular aspect of the Beverly Hills' essence that made an impression on me was the dizzying array of exotic automobiles zipping everywhere you turned. I reflexively maintained a mental record of twenty-seven Rolls Royce, sixteen Bentleys, and eleven limousines. Every other car was a Mercedes Benz or Jaguar—too numerous to count. Join me as I regale my experiences of driving, riding in, pushing, pulling, and even polishing some of the most exotic cars on the planet. Climb in, and give the driver the command … *Home, James!*

I Miss My Bentley

Before I moved to Los Angeles, I made a trip with my mother to scout out the neighborhoods to see if I really wanted to move. Via a connection in Indianapolis, I successfully contacted Alex Trebek and organized a visit to his home on Mulholland Drive. When Mom and I arrived at the house we found Alex in the garage dusting off a vintage Bentley coupe. He greeted us with a smile and a handshake and led us through garage into the house. As he was introducing us to his wife Elaine his mother emerged from a back hallway. The visit was short, and as we left I commented on the beautiful car. He remarked, "I love that car."

Several years later I bumped into Alex at the Polo Lounge in the Beverly Hills Hotel. I asked about Elaine and his aging mother.

"Elaine is fine," he replied. "My mother is now living on her own."

Then I asked about the Bentley.

"I sold the Bentley on the same day that my mother moved out of the house," he said, "and I sure do miss that Bentley."

Eviction Notice

My silver 1998 Cadillac DeVille was the last of a series of five cars gifted to me by Aunt Thelma. The other four were Lincoln Town Cars. I loved them, the Cadillac not so much. The entire time I owned the car it seemed that I was continually driving from one mechanic to the next. The final visit to a repairman was in Desert Hot Springs aka Desperate Hot Springs, an area of the desert best known for meth labs and ne'er-do-wells. After many futile calls to the mechanic, I was forced to make the twenty-minute drive to check the status of my lousy Cadillac.

When I arrived at the repair shop it was closed up tight and neither my car nor the mechanic where anywhere to be found. A loitering Latino told me in broken English, "He live down street," pointing due west of the shop. I ventured in the direction he pointed, and at the end of the poorly paved road found my Cadillac in a vacant dirt lot. Not only had Jorge failed to repair my car, he had taken up residence in it too! The car was unlocked. I took all of Jorge's shit and piled it in the open lot. Then I called AAA, and they came and hauled Jorge's house away. I borrowed a black marker from the tow-truck driver and wrote a note, "Your ass has been evicted!" and left it on the mound.

This Is Not My Car

Sir Charles Neave-Hill, the fourteenth master of Land's End England, came to visit. I met him at the Mondrian Hotel on Sunset Boulevard. After a night of heavy drinking Charles was insistent that we go out for an evening on the town. He was *nuts!*

He handed the valet a heavy tip and we climbed into his cedar-colored, right-hand drive Bentley and sped off into the night.

"Could you open the glove box and fetch my cell phone?" he asked.

I opened the glove box, no phone. Patting the center console he said, "Look in here." I popped it open and with a puzzled expression he looked inside. "Bloody hell, this isn't my fucking car!" he exclaimed. Then he dismissed it and continued on, "Not my problem. Let's go have some fun!"

When we finally returned to the hotel he turned the keys over with indifference. It turned out that Sir Charles was so hammered he forgot that his car wasn't even in this country!

Somebody Save My Rolls Royce

I was sick of getting screwed by mechanics. A friend recommended one in Hollywood that he claimed was reliable and had been there for half a century, "All the stars go there." Arriving at the shop, a guy came out and handed me a clipboard. I stepped inside the garage and saw Norm Crosby's two-tone blue Rolls Royce recognizing it by the license plate, "NORMC." Suddenly a mechanic bolted out of a bay yelling, "Call the fire department!" The garage rapidly began to fill with black smoke and I heard sirens. I saw a pegboard of keys just to my left and hastily grabbed the set with the tag that read Norm Crosby. I backed the Rolls Royce out and parked it safely in an adjacent lot just as the fire engines arrived. The funny thing is that I never heard from Norm again.

CHAPTER 10

Dinner Is ... Served

Throughout history, dining has played a foremost role in society. Royal feasts, wedding banquets, holiday dinners, and political fundraisers keep the masses busy stuffing their faces every day of the year. Business lunches render financial fact (or folly). Jewish Sabbath dinners warm the hearts of faithful followers. Jesus fed 5,000 with the miracle of the loaves and fish at Bethsaida and broke bread at the Last Supper.

I have wined and dined in eateries throughout the world, consuming stuff even Indiana Jones would push away. Divergent cultural eating habits and table etiquette are as remarkable as they are peculiar. Join me as I share amusingly engaging experiences as ... *Dinner Is ... Served.*

Who Changed the Fucking Place Cards?

Paula Stewart appeared in 1961 in a New York production of *Wildcat* with Lucille Ball, during which time she and Lucille became close friends. When I met Paula at the Bel Age Hotel in 1985, I found her so attractive and captivating that I immediately invited her to accompany me to a luncheon hosted by socialite Herbert Hischmoeller van Kamphuyzen in Beverly Hills.

When I went to collect Paula, I was surprised to learn that she was a guest-in-residence at Lucille Ball's home. At that afternoon luncheon, she invited me to a dinner party at Lucille Ball's. When I returned Paula to Lucy's house that afternoon, I noticed the Starline Tour Bus sitting at the curb. Paula had a striking resemblance to Lucy, so I said, "Let's have a little fun. Put on your sunglasses and wave!" She did and the tour bus roared rumbled with excitement.

The following weekend I went to Lucy's house for the much-anticipated soirée. I called before arriving, and Paula instructed me to enter through the side service door. She met me there and introduced me to the staff. We then walked through the dining room where Paula glanced at the place cards and seating arrangement. Paula was obviously displeased with the arrangement because she started shuffling the place cards. I questioned her action.

"Oh," she said, "She doesn't pay any attention. She lets the staff assign the seating." So I thought nothing more of it, as we proceeded to the drawing room to greet the other guests. Paula introduced me to Gary Morton and Mr. and Mrs. Jimmy Stewart. We slid into the conversation. Just as I was becoming comfortable, a guttural, booming voice came from the dining room, "Who changed the *fucking* place cards?"

Conversations stopped. The room went silent.

Lucille Ball entered the room with innate radiance dressed in a diaphanous black gown and wearing a diamond brooch the size of a Volkswagen. She graciously made her way around the room, greeting each and every guest with individual consideration. Paula stood as Lucy approached and introduced me. Basking in the excitement of the moment, I offered my hand and said, "Hello." Lucy smiled and acknowledged me with a nod. Lucy then leaned into Paula and in a stage whisper said, "Don't ever do that again."

Table for One

The Hamburger Hamlet on Sunset Boulevard was a popular dining spot throughout the 1980s for notables and common folk alike. Famous people could be seen dining there any given night of the week. Sunday night was popular. In fact, one Sunday in particular was outstanding. Lauren Bacall was in the corner booth opposite Lisa Hartman and Clint Black. Carole Cook was entertaining family at the front of the restaurant.

Dean Martin arrived in an oyster-colored Rolls Royce Corniche hardtop at precisely 6:35 p.m. While his driver opened the door in front of Hamburger Hamlet, as the hostess was removing a "reserved" sign from Dean's personal table. Mr. Martin seated himself, and the barkeeper delivered his customary Scotch on the rocks. Without presentation of the Hamlet's billboard-sized menu, Dean Martin would place his order, and then watch the television above the bar. He ate in silence, never speaking to anyone, not even the staff. Mid-meal, a second Scotch was delivered and an empty glass removed. At the end of the ceremonious evening, the Rolls Royce and driver reappeared at precisely 8:35 p.m., and Dean Martin exited as he entered, in complete silence.

After the third consecutive Sunday of observing this odd behavior, I approached Carole Cook to get her thoughts on Dean Martin's curious routine. She first noticed him at Hamburger Hamlet on a Sunday night soon after hearing that Dean Martin Jr. was killed in a plane crash.

"He's in here every Sunday," she said. "Even I'm afraid to talk to him."

Whenever I had out-of-town guests who wanted to see a movie star, it was a sure thing to find Dean Martin at Hamburger Hamlet … Sunday night … Table for one … Two scotches … Still mourning.

I Prefer a Bowl of Chili

To boost Christmas tree sales at the American Legion Post in Palm Springs, I asked Carole Channing to join me for a local CBS affiliate television interview. She kindly obliged. To thank her, I had arranged an early birthday luncheon for Carole's eighty-eighth birthday at a notable, upscale desert restaurant. Spencer's at the Palm Springs Tennis Club offered a superb menu with beef Wellington sliders, ahi tartare, and berries crème brûlée. As our party of six was en route, Carole abruptly announced, "What I'd really like is a bowl of chili at Bit of Country."

I made a hard U-turn in the middle of the street, and sped off for the notorious greasy spoon. Not only did I save three hundred bucks, but also had painful gas for days.

I Don't Grow It, I Don't Eat It

Eddie Albert was noted for his social and environmental activism. He promoted organic gardening and founded City Children's Farm for inner-city youth. He offered his Pacific Palisades home to a women's organization for a fundraiser in 1987.

When I arrived to play the function, I was surprised to find a cornfield concealing the front of his large Spanish-style house. In front of the healthy row of corn were multiple landscaped tiers in the rolling hillside property. Each tier was filled with hearty rows of various, unusually large vegetables.

For the most part, the luncheon was a bore. The ladies ensconced themselves in typical self-absorbed conversations and failed to relate to their eminent host who was reserved to the point of being withdrawn. When I introduced myself, I inquired about the gardens in front of the house. Albert reacted enthusiastically, taking me by the arm and leading me to the front yard—perhaps just as desperate as I to escape the prattling women. Once outside, the passionate gardener led me on a thorough tour of each row, and introduced me to each plant by name. A rhubarb named Gertrude looked down on the tier below where three oversized cabbages—Larry, Moe, and Curly—grew proudly. He explained that since his wife Margo passed in 1985 he found solace and comfort in this special garden.

Eddie Albert had a profound eccentricity—and a deep-love for the earth and nature. He enjoyed his home and spent most of his time there, rarely going to restaurants or events. Eddie was a wee phobic about dining out: "If I don't grow it, I don't eat it."

My Horses Took the Afternoon Off

For years I maintained a membership to the prestigious Turf Club at the Hollywood Park Race Track. When it opened in 1938, Harry Warner from Warner Brothers served as its chairman. Warner's 600 chair holders included vaudeville's Al Jolson and legendary silent film actor Raoul Walsh. The Turf Club offered white tablecloths and white-gloved dining to an elite group of private members. The club was arranged in open-air tiers for optimum viewing of the racetrack.

John Forsythe would sit in the tier directly below me. He intently followed the racing events—his table was always covered with racing forms and notepads. Forsythe's focus didn't waiver. Directly above me, the scene was quite the opposite. Tim Conway and Mel Brooks often shared a table where they were disruptively hilarious. The constant stream of jokes was interrupted only when Don Adams, Dick Martin, or Milton Berle stopped by to say hello.

I loved the club's sirloin steak and Caesar salad, but the jokes were the best part of the experience. Whenever anyone asked Tim Conway if he had horses in the race he would respond, "I arranged a poolside cabana for them at the Beverly Hills Hotel. They needed a day off."

Good times at The Turf Club. Sadly, the Fall Meet will conclude on December 22, 2013, ending Hollywood Park's seventy-five-year illustrious history.

A Little Somethin' for Supper

For many years an inconspicuous market was frequented by a variety of Beverly Hills residents. Located on the southeast corner of Santa Monica Boulevard and Doheny Drive, Carl's Market quietly served the community for nearly half of a century. The butcher, the baker, and the cashier offered tailored service to an elite clientele. I would sometimes stop by the market simply to check out their traditional items, indigenous only to the neighborhood markets.

One afternoon, while waiting in line to pay the cashier, an old woman standing in front of me was humming a melodic tune. I leaned around to look at her face and noticed that she was carrying music charts. I read the name printed at the top of the chart, Ella Fitzgerald. I put my hand on her shoulder and said, "Miss Fitzgerald?"

She slowly turned to look at me with affectionate eyes through heavy lensed glasses and said quietly, "Yes, baby?"

"I noticed your music charts and wanted to say hello" Here I was, standing near a living music legend. I was speechless. But she volunteered, "I just finished rehearsal at the Hollywood Bowl and thought that I would stop to get something for supper," motioning to the few grocery items in her arms. When she placed them on the counter I timidly asked her for an autograph. Ella Fitzgerald asked the cashier for a pen and reached for a brown paper bag. Many people may have an autograph from Ella Fitzgerald, but how many on a brown grocery bag … from Carl's Market?

Don't Give Up Hope

In 1990 I had the opportunity to play a New Year's celebration for Bob and Delores Hope at their iconic Volcano Home in Palm Springs. Pictured on postcards and visible only from the desert floor, the mysterious house always intrigued me. The $50 million, 23,000 square-foot architectural wonder had sweeping views of the entire Coachella Valley and was primarily a second residence—used for entertaining close friends and family. A grand piano was rented for the occasion and placed in the open atrium. The evening was brilliant.

A few years later, Bob and Delores Hope came into Lyons English Grille piano lounge. Discovering me at the grand, Bob and Delores issued an invitation for me to join them for dinner. Over prime rib and Yorkshire pudding, we became better acquainted. After dinner, they came back the piano lounge, and I performed a medley of songs ending with "Thanks for the Memories," Hope's theme song. A pat on the shoulder, a wink, and they were gone.

I was saddened to hear of Bob Hope's passing in 2003. I vividly recall a conversation with Father Don Merrifield, eleventh president of Loyola Marymount University, at a dinner party in Los Angeles. Father Don had referred to Bob and Delores as "aging," and added, "I certainly hope that she doesn't go first. If she does, we won't get a dime," the father continued, "She's very catholic. He is not!"

I Want My Menu Back!

During my two-week engagement at the fashionable Hotel Bel Air, nine members of the original *Star Trek* cast attended a rap party for *Star Trek VI*. I approached the table and introduced myself, and asked William Shatner for an autograph.

"I'll do better than that. Give me a few minutes," he said. Shatner grabbed a menu from a nearby table and passed it around to the cast. When I returned some time later, he handed me the menu with nine cast members' signatures on it. I thanked him for the prized memorabilia and returned to the piano. Throughout the evening I shared my treasure and proudly displayed it on the piano. Shortly before closing, my attorney friend Ronald J. Palmieri approached the piano, took one look at the autographed menu, and snatched it. Ron glared at me with menacing eyes and said, "I'll take this in lieu of payment for free legal counsel!" And this is why we all hate lawyers!

You Can't Pick Your Neighbors

When I was visiting my friend Philip Buck at St. John's Hospital in Los Angeles, I was intrigued to find out that the famous Broadway composer Jerry Herman was recuperating in the room next door. They were both rehabilitating from complications of HIV in the early '90s. After commiserating, they became close friends. Philip introduced me.

Six months later, Jerry Herman invited me to his home (Dinah Shore's former estate) in Palm Springs for dinner. I made the unfortunate mistake of taking Rick, a devilishly handsome paramour, as my guest. Rick captivated Herman's attention. We enjoyed a poolside candlelit dinner of baked artichokes and veal chops. Alcohol was involved. Before the evening was over, Jerry and Rick exchanged phone numbers and were making plans. The following day, Jerry called and invited me for lunch at his home in Bel Air. Uniformed maids and servants served luncheon in the garden solarium. During the meal, Jerry questioned me about Rick to the point of distraction. Later we toured Jerry's museum of memorabilia in the basement of the mansion.

I left the estate with mixed emotions. The mistake of introducing Rick to Jerry all but destroyed my relationship with Jerry Herman. The moral of the story: Be careful whom you take to dinner!

CHAPTER 11

Dames!

Females are fascinating creatures. They can be perilously enthralling and persuasively menacing whereas they are insufferably essential to a man's existence. Heterosexual men desire them. Homosexual men want to be them. Beautiful … unassailable … imperious … captivating … Whatever! They're all … *Dames!*

"O" My!

My first Lincoln Town Car was a 1988 Cartier Series, gunmetal gray. Its initial trip to the Santa Palm Car Wash was comical. When I arrived I was reluctant to turn the keys over for fear that the employees might scratch it before it went through the wash. I left my prized new possession in their trusty hands, paid for the car wash, and waited at the other end for my baby to emerge. As the gleaming grill came into view, I swelled with excitement and looked to see if anyone else was watching. The car slowly moved forwards inch-by-inch … by inch … by foot … by foot … what the hell? What happened? They stretched my car! Coincidentally, my car was directly behind an identical gunmetal gray model stretch limousine. Wow. What a sight!

I proudly drove my sparkling new Town Car to the Beverly Hills Hotel to attend a reception for Michael Crawford of *The Phantom of the Opera* fame. After the event, the valet area was inundated with people waiting for their cars to be brought around. As I passed through the front doors of the hotel, I glanced to my left and noticed a woman with an open briefcase sitting alone on the banquet. Just as I was looking at her, she raised her head. It was Jacqueline Onassis. Without missing a step, I continued to the end of the red carpet and handed my parking ticket to the attendant. Out of the crowd appeared my friend, former Miss America contestant, Marilyn Watson. I kissed her on the cheek and whispered, "Did you see Jacqueline Onassis sitting back there?"

She smiled and quietly returned, "She's standing right behind you."

I turned abruptly and extended my hand. "I've admired you. I am Jere Ring."

She smiled, shook my hand and softly said, "I'm Jacqueline Onassis." Well, duh! All eyes remained on Mrs. Onassis as the parade of cars continued to arrive.

I pointed out my new Lincoln Town Car to Marilyn as the valet pulled the car up. She congratulated me and as I hugged her and bid farewell, Marilyn looked over my shoulder.

"Are you sure that is your car?"

Confused, I said, "Yes. Why?"

"Well …" she giggled, "if it is, Mrs. Onassis just got into your car." I stepped off the curb and looked at the license plate. Yes, it was my car. Directly behind mine, an identical Lincoln Town Car was in the queue. Jacqueline Onassis' driver stepped out of her car. I looked at him. He looked at me. The valet looked at him looking at me. We all looked at each other in a quandary: What do we do? Sensing the confusion, the crowd quieted. I went to the passenger door, opened it and said, "Mrs. Onassis … I believe you are in the wrong car."

She ran her hand across the seat and said, "Oh, you are right. My car doesn't have leather seats." I offered my hand; she accepted and gracefully rose from the car and slipped her arm through mine as I walked her back to her car. I opened the door; she set her briefcase inside, sat down, and swung her legs in.

I leaned down and said, "It was a pleasure meeting you, Mrs. Onassis."

"It was nice meeting you, Mr. Ring." I had only mentioned my name one time, and she remembered it. (After that, I wrote to her New York address, and sent her two letters and a postcard.)

About eight months later, I was performing on the *Radisson Diamond* and sailed into St. Kitts, where my friend Gwenny Fisk-Halleran had a huge oceanfront home in Dieppe Bay. When she found out I was coming, she invited friends over for cocktails. When she answered the door, I looked across the room and saw someone who looked like Jacqueline Onassis.

"Is that Jackie Onassis?"

"Yes, it is." Gwenny said. "I'll introduce you in a few minutes." When she left, I made a beeline for Mrs. Onassis.

When I said hello, Mrs. Onassis excused herself from the conversation she was having, and once again slipped her arm in mine. We began to walk and settled upon a settee in the living room. It amazed me that she still remembered my name.

God Bless Aunt Thelma

I loved my Aunt Thelma, not because she gave me four Lincoln Town Cars and a Cadillac, a house in Palm Springs, and put me through prep school ... I just plain loved her! Thelma Moore was elegant, strikingly beautiful, and sweet. She also played the piano and sang ... Imagine that!

My uncle Harry married her for all the same reasons I loved her, and he loved her, too. After five wives, he finally found his treasure in Aunt Thelma. Harry did not care that her Aunt Violet managed a brothel and Aunt Ethel ran off with the circus. Mom and dad reluctantly shared a story about spotting Thelma leaving a gentleman's apartment at 7am one Sunday morning before church. She remained an angel to me!

Harry died when I was fifteen, and I moved in with Thelma for three months. She bought my first grand piano and encouraged me to play. She took me to Starlight Musicals to see Liberace when I was eight. We traveled together—sharing a cabin on cruises, venturing to the Grand Hotel on Mackinac Island in the summers. Aunt Thelma even introduced me to California. I loved my Aunt Thelma.

The Rue de Vallée

When crooner Rudy Vallée died, his wife Eleanor was left destitute. She was trying desperately to sell the "Rue de Vallée their mansion in the Hollywood Hills. I went to visit Eleanor late one afternoon and found her in a very solemn state. She told me to go to "the museum" under the tennis courts and pick out whatever souvenir I wanted. The space had floor-to-ceiling industrial shelving jammed with everything that Rudy ever owned. Piles of shoes, ties and other clothing littered the floor. I picked up a postcard here and a book there. As I dug through the rubble, I discovered an old suitcase. Inside I found a large ventriloquist dummy and documentation. Upon returning to the house, I shared the find with Eleanor. I told her that she should have it appraised; it could be worth big money.

A year later, I saw Eleanor. She said the Charlie McCarthy doll sold for a large sum of money, and she was able to make improvements on the house, which was sold to Arsenio Hall. I guess it pays to be a pack rat. I was the jerk with the quirk that missed the perk.

To The Manor Born

Robertine Buchanan Fairbanks Daniels was the quintessence of elegance. The Queen Mum was her secret role model. She preserved the image without fail. Her wardrobe consisted of an infinite collection of signature coatdresses that were meticulously fashioned with exquisite fabrics by a personal dressmaker that she boasted to have "pinched" from the Royal Family. A pair of matching Cartier platinum and diamond bracelets always dangled on her wrists. Three graduated strands of superb pearls displayed a glittering diamond clip to the lower left of her chin. Her preferred fragrance was Shalimar, which she claimed to have worn since 1921 when it was created by Jacques Guerlain, and exclusive only to Parisian shoppers. She lived and thrived during an era when American aristocracy knew no bounds. Robertine always was and will be one of my most favorite people in life! She was intriguing, eccentric and unpredictable.

Robertine's was married to Richard Monroe Fairbanks whose father, Charles Warren Fairbanks, was a former Vice President of the United States. When Richard Fairbanks died in 1944, she married Joe Daniels, a prominent attorney in Indianapolis. A classmate introduced me to Mrs. Daniels shortly after I graduated from prep school. Irving, her chauffeur of 35 years was aging and found it difficult to walk, much less drive. Irving happily joined the household staff after I became her new driver.

For several years, Mrs. Daniels grandly rode in the back seat of the '61 Cloud Rolls Royce. After a short while, she found herself more comfortable in the front seat next to me. She was thrilled to relive her illustrious past with me and I was very happy to listen. "As a young lady, it was in poor taste to leave the dance floor, unsupervised, with a young man." As time passed, she began to share stories of more intimate nature. Her marriage to Richard Fairbanks was spent in separate beds. Soon after she married Joe Daniels, he suffered a stroke and was confined to a wheelchair. For many years, her only romantic liaisons were with Barbara Cartland romance novels.

I was very aware that Mrs. Daniels was distraught when I decided to move to California. We both effectively concealed our emotions. On the day that I went to her house to say goodbye, she asked me for one last favor. She said, "I've never seen an erect penis." So I showed her mine.

CHAPTER 12

Euro Snobs

Marbella is a city in Andalusia, Spain, by the Mediterranean. It sits beneath La Concha in the province of Málaga. The surrounding area is a popular beach resort playground for the rich and famous on the Costa del Sol, a favorite destination for wealthy tourists and prominent international celebrities. I spent the summer of 1986 in this indulgently magnificent resort, basking in the sun and soaking up the culture. Not to my surprise, I got caught up with the obnoxiously wealthy jet set international society. This is a diminutive subculture that ebbs and flows with radical unpredictability similar to the currents in the Mediterranean Sea itself. Allow me to introduce you to the titles of Europe, aristocratic heirs, social climbers and dregs alike that make up the culture of … *Euro Snobs*.

Baron and Baroness von Trousers

Puerto Banús was bustling in the summer of 1986. Arab oil money had restructured the social makeup of the Mediterranean coast. For generations, the French Riviera and the Costa del Sol has been reputedly popular as a playground for the rich, and with the introduction of exorbitantly obvious new money, the evidence of extravagant wealth was never greater than in the mid-1980s. The outstanding creations of mega-yacht king Bharat Paolo Vitelli could be seen in every port.

The flat in which I lived for that summer was located on the second floor of a luxury building overlooking the larger, more imposing private vessels that were moored closest to the entrance of the harbor. An ever-changing array of magnificent floating palaces were secured to the shore and anchored bow outward, parallel to one another they lined the perimeter of the harbor. Many times I would contentedly sit on the terrace, sipping a morning cappuccino, and survey the activity on the open-air esplanade and narrow access road below.

The busy gradually rotating in the middle of the tiny harbor, attaining proper positioning to back into the vacant spot on the promenade directly in front of me. I watched a gleaming white craft at least two hundred feet in length with a modestly sized helicopter resting amidships on a small square-landing pad. Crewmembers scurried around the open decks as the captain barked commands from an open fly bridge. A pewter Bentley sedan arrived as the vessel was being backed into its berth. With mechanical precision, the passenger gangway gradually extended to the shore. A large sliding glass door then opened on the lower aft deck and two dark, bearded Arab men emerged and ambled down the gangway. Female counterparts, cloaked in black Islamic hijab veiling, followed. Without words, the group climbed into the car that slowly drove away. I was quite fascinated by the scenario. It's amazing what luxuries the sale of a few million barrels of oil can buy.

My stay in Puerto Banús came about by way of an invitation

from Kate McAloon, a beautiful young lady who was the former manager of a very posh Beverly Hills nightclub-restaurant called the Excelsior where I performed in the penthouse of the Rodeo Collection on Rodeo Drive. It was by far one of the more elegant rooms I have ever played.

When the restaurant closed in the spring of 1984, Kate left Los Angeles to study at Le Cordon Bleu Cooking School in France. It was there she met and began a relationship with Albert Vince, a successful businessman who had recently sold a large chain of supermarkets in the UK for a very large sum of money. He had allegedly taken his golden earnings, evaded taxes, and skipped out on Parliament. He went into exile on the Costa del Sol and purchased a massive home in the fashionable hillsides of Marbella. Kate accompanied Albert to the south of Spain, and when asked by Albert what she wanted for her birthday, she replied, "A nightclub!"

Kate's club, Spirit of Ecstasy, opened in the high summer season of 1986. Hand-painted panels, etched mirrors, and erotic furnishings graced the stage at the center of the large room. A wooden statue of the Mistress of Ecstasy stood majestically at the center of the venue. One could almost feel her presence as she presided over the crowds below, her eyes fixed on the horizon beyond the yacht harbor. A grand piano was placed directly below the face of the statue and was supported by three carved locks of the Mistress' hair that curled upward from the floor. The club was one gigantic work of art, fashioned according to precise measurements and delivered by transport from Italy where they were created by a handful of commissioned artisans. I had fortunately been misinformed about the club's opening date and arrived six weeks early, making it possible for me to experience the entire composition.

During those six weeks, Kate and I skated in and around the social scene of Marbella. Ronald Reagan had dropped a bomb on Muammar al-Gaddafi in Libya on April 15. So in the wake of disturbing media coverage, American tourists were few, which made Kate's and my presence exclusive. Kate was the spokesperson for Moët & Chandon White Star Champagne for the region, and her title, of course, became a magnet for invitations to dinners, luncheons, and countless functions, and who better to escort her than my little ole fabulous self!

Our first invitation out of the social hat was for luncheon at El Rincón. This massive estate was the summer home of the Baron Hubert and Baroness Terry von Pantz (or as I referred to them, "Baron and Baroness von Trousers"). Hubert, a titled Austrian, and Terry, the CEO and principal stockholder of Avon Cosmetics, made a powerful pair. He had the title, and she had the bucks. Together, they kicked some major social butt! I found it difficult at first to acclimate to the social schedule in Marbella. Dinner was usually served around 10:00 p.m. The discos never really got hopping before 2:00 a.m. One would go to bed—that is, if they did go to bed—just after sunup. Breakfast was basically nonexistent. Luncheon would be leisurely served anywhere between 3:00 and 5:00 p.m. Because she could, the Baroness von Pantz frequently bent the rules and insisted that her guests arrive around 1:00 p.m. Kate and I called early and she, being familiar with the many faces of Euro-society, clued me in on the "who was, is, and what for" of the fifty-something invited guests as they began to arrive. The guest list read like an imperious society write-up from *Town and Country Magazine.*

Prince Alfonso of Hohenlohe-Langenburg, esteemed proprietor of the famed Marbella Club, was chatting with London's Countess of Dudley in the foyer when we arrived. Billionaire Greek shipping tycoon Stavros Niarchos ambled in on our heels with Princess Firyal of Jordan on his arm. I struck up a conversation with a most-distinguished gentleman on the terrace. When I introduced myself, he graciously bowed, and spoke in a Parisian-French dialect. My expression of bewilderment caught the attention of a ravishingly beautiful redhead who translated the introduction, revealing Baron Guy Édouard Alphonse Paul de Rothschild. The redhead was Linda Christian, the international film star made famous for having once married Tyrone Power. Marta Oyarzabal Lodge (whose father was the late John Cabot Lodge, the American Ambassador to Switzerland) was seated with her husband at our table. Following the introduction to Princess Johanna zu Sayn-Wittgenstein who was seated next to Princess Marie-Louise of Prussia (great granddaughter of Kaiser Wilhelm II) who, with her husband Count Rudolf "Rudi" von Schonburg-Glauchau dominated the conversation at the table. I began to get lightheaded.

By the time dessert was served, I was going dippy attempting to keep up with the grandness of the tête-à-tête. I left the central open-air terrace where the luncheon was being served and wandered down a long expansive corridor, popping my head into open doors to inspect rooms along the way.

A cozy antechamber led into a sizable gallery with dark paneled walls that held a disturbing collection of wild animal trophy heads that I assumed the Baron had collected from his many hunting expeditions. Another room boasted floor-to-ceiling bookshelves that surrounded an array of card tables. Members of the fourteen-member staff who were not tending to the luncheon were fluffing pillows and placing clean pads and sharpened pencils on tables awaiting avid bridge players. I stepped through the broad archway at the end of the hall into the grand drawing room. A life-size portrait of the Baron and Baroness was on a distant wall, and comfortable couches and overstuffed chairs composed multiple conversation areas. A lengthy wall of glass provided a spectacular view of the Mediterranean Sea through the stand of Lebanon pines on the rolling lawns. Much to my delight, I discovered a piano in the far left corner of the room! I was excited. A very large piano!! I became more excited. A very large bright crimson Steinway ten foot concert grand piano!!! I was thrilled!

I looked around the room. No staff. No guests. Perfect! I sat down and began to play. I started with a very soft rendition of Debussy, "Claire de Lune"; and gradually moved into Rachmoninoff, *Rhapsody on a Theme of Paganini*. As I was playing, I could sense the presence of someone moving behind me. I continued to play, assuming it was one of the staff. I completed Rhapsody with an affective arpeggio, folded my hands in my lap, and raised my head to take in the spectacular view before me. I was suddenly startled by the sound of a resounding basso voice that broke the silence of the expansive room.

"Do you know any Cole Porter?" The voice demanded.

When I turned to see who was delivering this profound query, I was both intrigued and amused. The Baron von Pantz, flanked by a pair of golden labs, was sitting in a stately chair directly behind me.

"You are a wonderful pianist," he remarked in a genuine tone. "Please, continue." He paused for a moment and then reiterated in a more compassionate tone, "Do you know any Cole Porter?"

"I do indeed," I responded with pride and began to cheerfully play and sing, "*The night is young, the skies are clear, and if you want to go walkin' dear … It's delightful, it's delicious, it's delovely.*"

I meandered through "Night and Day," "Under My Skin," and "Miss Otis Regrets." Much to my absolute delight, by the time I was crooning "True Love" and "In the Still of The Night," the room began to fill with guests. The Baron had instructed one of the staff to open the windows on the east wall, allowing the melodies to float into the group on the terrace.

"Love For Sale!"

My enthusiasm grew.

"What Is This Thing Called Love?"

The guests began to sing along.

When I broke into, "What A Swell Party This Is," the Baron and Baroness began to dance around the room. When I finished the song, the regal couple bowed to the guests' roaring applause, then came directly to the piano to offer their thanks and congratulate me on a job well done. The Baroness delivered a friendly invitation and an unyielding appeal for me and a guest to attend all events henceforth for the season at her home. I accepted her gracious offer as the Baron chimed in, prophetically expressing one stipulation:

"You must play for your supper!" It was a spirited demand. I acknowledged it, knowing it would be my pleasure, by playing one of my favorite, whimsical Cole Porter tunes, "Let's Misbehave." The regal couple smiled.

Queen of the Night

I first met French singer and nightclub impresaria Régine in Beverly Hills. What a bitch! I had no idea who she was, but I knew that she had to be someone big, as she was traveling in the company of Julio Iglesias. When we were introduced at Villa El Rincón, neither one of them acknowledged my extended hand. With complete lack of respect, they dismissed me. When Régine began to faun over me at the piano, I ignored her. Now it was my turn to be the bitch.

The Red and Black Ball

I attended some spectacular parties in Marbella on the Costa del Sol during the summer of 1986. Prince Alfonso von Hohenlohe, the founder of the Marbella Club, generally set the pace with outrageous themes that were vividly designated on elaborate hand delivered invitations. I answered the door of my flat in Puerto Banús one afternoon to pleasantly discover a well-muscled messenger, deliciously clad in cellophane. He was delivering, what else, an invitation to the Cellophane Ball! The costume requirement for the evening was something creative … in cellophane. And creative they were indeed. Multitudes of hidden secrets were exposed at that bash.

I escorted Shirley Bassie to another themed soirée, The Red and Black Ball. I wore red from my shirt to my shoes and carried a black Labrador puppy as my counter-color. The pup was the most popular with the paparazzi.

Nobility Runs Amuck

Titled people are in abundance in Los Angeles. The streets run rampant with barons, counts, and the occasional princess or marquis.

Renowned Beverly Hills socialite, Contessa Cohn's birth name was Alice. The self-appointed aristocratic flamboyance of her "noble" title was inconsistent with her distinctive diaphanous gowns and overly sweet manner. But she pulled off the spurious masquerades with overwhelming success. Her ostentatious social gatherings, though tawdry, were ardently lauded.

A "Blue Book" socialite friend introduced me to Egyptian Prince Rahid Ghali. I researched his ancestry but was only able to uncover unfounded information that he was the alleged nephew of Princess Faiza Fouad Rauf, sister of Egypt's last monarch. I met Faiza on a number of occasions but never found opportunity to pursue the issue. She was purportedly ensconced in intimate relations with Prince Ali Kahn at the time so I maintained a precautionary distance.

He had a penchant for pricey cognac, specifically Louis XIII Remy Martin Grande Champagne Cognac, which falls off the shelves for about $2,000 a bottle. I discovered and confiscated an empty Baccarat Crystal decanter in its elegant satin-lined signature red box from a dusty shelf at the Excelsior Restaurant in Beverly Hills. I filled the graceful vessel with cheap Paul Masson VSOP Grande Amber Brandy for color, and placed it on my bar. His nibs, the Prince went into an outburst of rapture upon discovering the signature crystal decanter. I gave him a stylish Tiffany crystal snifter, and he spent the evening in ecstasy, never realizing that he was headed for a debilitating wino's hangover the next morning.

The Baron Frederick von Soosten introduced me to Countess Cis Zoltowska at one of his notorious parties. I can still see her perched like an ingénue in the corner of the drawing room. Her jet-black hair pulled into a tight chignon. She wore heavy dark orange makeup. Colossal false lashes were hooded by exaggeratedly black painted eyebrows, and a fuchsia-colored silk mini dress exposed her splotchy leg makeup. Lime-colored fingernails coordinated with brightly colored rings and bangle bracelets that matched chains around her neck. I was drawn to her immediately. Shortly after I was introduced, she timidly shared that she grew up in Austria and met and married an indigent Polish count in Switzerland during the Second World War. She began making jewelry in the 1950s and as I understand, her designs are world-renowned today. My favorite thing about Countess Cissy was that she smoked cigars.

The Marquis de Yzbek looked like he popped off of the pages of a Harry Potter novel. His long graying shoulder length hair emphasized an extended goatee. On his gold trimmed velvet jacket he typically wore a collection of jeweled pins that he claimed were awards for noble valor from various titled heads of Europe. Ruffled lace flowed from his shirt collar and cuffs. His fingers, with the nails grown long and painted faint gold, displayed overly large rings. The most obvious fashion statement of the enigmatic marquis were red heeled, pointed toed, satin bowed shoes. He claimed to be a direct decent of King Louis XIV of France and chose to carry on the mid-seventeenth century tradition that only those in royal favor were allowed the privilege of wearing red heels on their shoes. It was quite a look. The Marquis traveled with his companion, the Baron Franz who claimed to have grown up in a chateau. He was of noble German heritage from the House of Saxe-Weimar-Eisenach. I traced him as far as Bayard, West Virginia, population 281 where farmhouses by far outnumber chateaus in that particular region.

Of all the self-appointed nobility that I have met through the years, the prizewinner is Baron Frederick von Soosten. Upon our initial introduction, I commented on the hefty diamond like studs that ever so ostentatiously graced the placket of the baron's pleated white formal shirt. He stridently claimed that they were priceless gems that were extracted from a centuries old tiara that belonged to his mother, the late Baroness Margaret von Soosten. They were paste, of course. The truth later revealed itself that his mother and his father were the groundskeepers for the Baroness' estate in La Jolla, California. They were tragically killed on the property and being of noble blood, the baroness adopted Freddy out of pity. She was the former wife of Edward Schweitzer, whose father was the alleged head of the Bayer Aspirin Company. She left nothing to Fred when she died in 1974.

The Baron and his partner, Bill Green, lived in a shoebox-sized two-bedroom apartment on the fifth floor of the less-than-desirable La Brea Apartments in Los Angeles. The tiny domicile was crammed with foreboding|y massive period furniture and object d'art. The baron once described a grand four-poster bed that was jammed into a tiny bedroom as belonging to Marie Antoinette. Bill, his partner, corrected him. He revealed that they picked it up at a snappy garage sale.

Bill was an affable gentleman whom the baron referred to as his "black man" and frequently attempted to pass him off as his chauffeur, butler, or personal valet, whichever designation the present situation warranted. Bill would shrug his shoulders and grant the overly inflated baron his fantasy. I never saw the alleged yacht that was anchored somewhere along the coast. I was however offered a ride in the antiquated two-tone gold-and-cedar-colored Rolls Royce that boldly boasted the von Soosten coat of arms on the front doors. The "black man" drove. The baron and I sat in the back. I did hear in later years that a former wealthy lover of the "black man" had died and left Bill a massive fortune. When I heard of Bill's luck, I wondered who was driving and who is riding in the back of the Rolls now?

CHAPTER 13

Quirks, Jerks, and Perks

The Latin word *eccentricus* translates as "out of center," and for me, the farther off center, the better. My neighbor, Helen Hamilton, used to say, "I like interesting people because I'm interesting." Even her *hair* was interesting! She was eccentric.

Bizarre people catch my attention. Twisted people inspire me! Life is too short to chitchat at the country club. Go have a hot dog at Costco and meet some real people! With Quirks and Jerks, there are loads of Perks!

Eugene

At first I thought Eugene was the official maintenance man for the warehouse that I leased near the Palm Springs Airport. And then I found out he was a homeless guy who was allowed to live there to keep an eye on the place and occasionally pick up a broom. I shared the 40,000-square-foot structure with a company that manufactured million-dollar coaches. I filled my half with a $7 million inventory of mainframe computer equipment that I had purchased for pennies on the dollar from the Morton Thiokol Incorporated in Brigham City, Utah. In about a ten-month period, I eventually sold the equipment to a variety of buyers from around Southern California. During that time, Eugene and I became friends. He would occasionally ask me if I could spot him a five or a ten. I never refused. I trusted him.

When the last of the equipment was sold, I closed the temporary business, vacated the warehouse, and began performing in a local piano bar in Palm Springs. One evening, my old buddy Eugene showed up with hair cut and combed; he was wearing army fatigue pants a white dress shirt. I was very pleased to see him again. He shook my hand, took a seat at a nearby table, and ordered a drink. He didn't stay long and as he left he dropped a curious white envelope in the tip jar. On a break, I opened the envelope to find $135 cash and a handwritten account of the dates and amounts of every dollar I gave him. Eugene is the only person to whom I have given or loaned money in my life who paid me back.

Eugene was a character of golden scope. He was generous and obliging to a fault but not to be crossed or worse, double-crossed. He had a fiery temper and was a fighter. He was a Vietnam Vet, a diminutive pup with a pit bull disposition. In the wake of numerous unfortunate events, Eugene was forced to develop an ardent flair for homeless living. He maintained a number of storage units in various locations around the desert. He owned a decked out bicycle and trailer that he used to transport everything from camping gear to animals. He sought refuge in a variety of locations but typically subsisted in vacant buildings with the consent of the landlord. In 2000, he stayed in my home for ten months while I traveled the world. He paid meticulous attention to my precious pooches and maintained my property. One incident necessitated the use of his trusty crossbow. The intruder truly regretted his choice of objective.

Eugene moved his mother from Diamond Bar, California, to the desert in 1992 and placed her in a studio apartment in Cathedral City where she lived for ten years. He worked as a night-shift janitor at a popular deli-restaurant, and saved as much money as he could outside of caring for his mother. Shortly after her death in 2002, he won a long battle with the VA and was granted his military benefits, and hit a $10,000 jackpot at the Spa Casino. He pulled his parts together, dissolved his storage unit assets and made tracks to Hawaii.

Eugene now lives in a unique home on the big island. He creatively connected three shipping containers and outfitted them with his "creature comforts." He is one of my friends I most admire. Ready the guest room, Eugene! I'm coming to visit.

Sweet Mystery Of Life

Naomia Jean Sweet was one of the most captivating women that I have ever met. She was a classy dame. I met her shortly after her husband, Lem Sweet, put a gun in his mouth in the master bedroom of their Palos Verdes estate. The houseman discovered Lem Sweet's body while Naomia was out shopping. The authorities determined that it was suicide, the mess was cleaned up and that night Mrs. Sweet slept in the very room where her husband took his life earlier that day. Naomia claimed that the mafia had put out a hit on them and Lem took his own life to protect hers. I think he killed himself to get away from her. There was no other way out.

Shortly after I met Mrs. Sweet in Beverly Hills she disappeared. I was told that she had taken up with a cult in Washington State. I had no idea who Ramtha was but she did. She relocated to an area within close proximity to Yelm were the Ramtha School of Enlightenment was headquartered. J.Z. Knight who claimed to channel a 35,000-year-old warrior whose teachings enthralled scores of followers seeking to create their own destiny organized the school.

In the wake of a spiritual epiphany, Naomia returned to Beverly Hills and bought a home in Cold Water Canyon. She immediately began extensive remodeling on the house. At great expense she had the contractors dynamite the side of the hill to accommodate a garage. When the garage was complete she decided that it was too dark and had them add a pricey, giant glass cupola. On the corners of the house she placed convex mirrors. When the contractors finally asked what they were for she told them, "To guide aliens in for landings."

After the house was completed she decided to sell it and move to the desert. She bought a beautiful home in Rancho Mirage and brought "the ghosts" with her. Naomia Jean began to lose car keys and misplace expensive jewelry, and she explained the mishaps by saying, "The entities will not leave me alone."

She invited me to accompany her to the Integratron (Google it!) in Landers, California, for a sound bath. While we were there we visited the alleged alien landing fields. Naomia Jean claimed to have had a spiritual "walk-in" and changed her name to Andraya, which greatly confused her old friends. Andraya told her brother's family (she had no children) that Aunt Jean was gone. Her body had been taken over by another soul.

Regardless of her proclivities I enjoyed her company. I enjoyed it so much that I even asked her to marry me. I invited her to join me on world cruises while I was traveling with my show. We made glamorous appearances at fundraisers, parties, and receptions. She introduced me to her family and I introduced her to mine. Before wedding bells could ring, whatever-her-name-is-this-month started getting *really* weird. On numerous occasions my partner Johnny and I had to rescue Andraya from a local pub when she was too intoxicated to drive. When we finally got her back home and Johnny perched her on the edge of her bed she slurred, "This is unforgivable." Johnny pointed to a tattered, faded plastic bamboo tree in the corner of the room and replied, "That's unforgivable. You're fine."

More recently she started accusing me of leaving the sliding glass doors open at her house so that Johnny could "slip by security" and rob her. Andraya frequently called the police to report that she had an intruder. On one particular evening she left a desperate message on my voicemail. Fearing the worst, I called the police. They entered the home and found her intoxicated in the bedroom with furniture and statuary knocked over throughout the home. She claimed "the entities" did it.

I had to finally distance myself from Andraya when she accused me of stealing a cloisonné vase from her foyer. I became part of an investigation after she reported me to the Riverside County Sheriff. In turn, I threatened to file a lawsuit for slander and our thirty-year friendship came abruptly to an end. Oddly enough, I still love her and miss her. She was one of my most adored quirks with loads of perks.

Peaches

Whenever Johnny and I visit Ketchikan, Alaska, we make certain to drop by the Arctic Bar, a neighborhood watering hole that is owned by a heavy set gal named Paula whose mouth could make a freight train take a dirt road. Paula whips up the best Bloody Marys imaginable, and if you're hungry, she'll order you a greasy double cheeseburger from the Burger Queen across the street. We would use her Dodge Ram pickup truck (with gun rack) to run errands around town.

You could always count on regulars Double D and Peaches to be sitting at the bar. The two bearded codgers could sit and shoot the breeze for hours, sharing riveting stories with strangers whenever they could get the chance. Peaches had his name engraved on a brass plaque on the back of his barstool. When I asked if Peaches was someone special, Paula shouted, "*Heeelll* no! Nobody wants to sit in his fucking barstool. Shit, he can't hold his goddamn bladder." Paula was a real charmer.

Mind Your Elbows

English actress Hermione Baddeley, best known for her role as the maid in Mary Poppins, loved her gin. The first time she came to one of my Hollywood parties she said "hello" to me when I opened the door and then bolted for the bar and ordered a drink. By the time I caught up with her, Hermione was entertaining a group at the buffet. When I was finally able to interrupt her chattering I said, "Hermione, your left elbow is in the artichoke dip." She stood erect, licked her elbow and exclaimed, "Delicious!" and continued with her stories.

Hermione's favorite dining spot was the Cock and Bull, a popular restaurant on Sunset Boulevard. One evening she asked for a doggie bag. When the maitre 'd refused her, she scraped the remains of her roast beef and mashed potatoes into her open handbag. I still wonder if the leftovers were for her or the dog.

At a Christmas party she hung her full-length sable coat on the back of her chair. Another guest joined us at the table. When we stood to leave the party Hermione discovered that the leg of the chair of the guest next to her had pinned the tail of her coat. Rather than asking the guest to move his chair, she gave the coat a good yank and ripped open the back. In her characteristic bumbling manner she asked the hostess for a needle and thread. Hermione sat down to sew the coat back together and realized upon completing the task that she had sewn the coat to her dress and chose to wear the coat for the remainder of the evening.

The following weekend we attended yet another holiday party. Hermione brought out a moth-eaten cashmere cape edged with sable tails. As the evening progressed the tails fell off one by one. When I took Hermione home that night, I handed her a paper grocery bag filled with the tails.

I'm a Man!

Severyn Ashkenazy was a successful hotelier in West Hollywood. He was also a European gentleman. Skip E. Lowe, popular Hollywood TV host, was a funny little androgynous man. When I introduced the two at the Bel Age Hotel, Skip extended his hand to shake and Severyn raised it to kiss it. Skip screeched, "I'm a man! I'm a man!" To this day, I'm not so sure what he is.

Ring Zings Bing

Jeff and Rick Dudum moved into Coachella Valley like an invasive cancer. With Kathryn Crosby's blessing they built Bing Crosby's Restaurant and Piano Bar in a prime location in Rancho Mirage. It was my misfortune when the Dudums hired me to open the piano bar. My yearlong contract was for seven nights a week but met its end after just three weeks when the management claimed that I did not know how to play "Rat Pack" music. Cole Porter? George Gershwin? "No!" they exclaimed, "Frank Sinatra and Dean Martin." The transplants from Walnut Creek were ignorant to the fact that I was naming the composers. The real problem was that their minimal seating could not accommodate the large numbers of my following fans. Bing's was quickly becoming Ring's and they did not want that.

Shortly after I was "fired" I took the Dudums to court for breach of contract. When they continued to use my name and likeness for publicity I added charges for misrepresentation and false advertising. The lawsuit hung in the balance for two years until the judge finally ruled in my favor. Winning the judgment was easy while collecting the money was not. After I hired a collection agency, the Dudums seemed to change their corporate name as often as I changed my underwear. Shortly after I was able to collect my money the entire chain of restaurants systemically collapsed due to tax evasion.

The Spice Queen

The Baron Herbert Hischemoeller van Kamphuyzen was born to Dutch nobility. His wealth emanated from massive holdings in the spice industry. We called him "The Spice Queen." He and his partner Mark Nixon designed and built the Kasteel Kamphuyzen in Beverly Hills. For years they entertained in a grand manner. Whenever they went out in public they always invited wealthy heiress friend Eleanor Rudolph. The well-heeled trio was often seen arriving in the Baron's long-wheelbase Silver Rolls Royce Wraith touring car. Herbert's funeral in 1991 was a four hour-long spectacle. I sang *Ave Maria* from the balcony.

After Mark sold the Kasteel he and his new partner purchased a twenty-two-bedroom estate in Mexico and transformed it into an exclusive bed and breakfast. Rancho Cuernavaca hosted countless celebrities over the years. Mark was never seen without his large macaw on his shoulder. Tensions developed between Mark and the new boyfriend. The maid found Mark murdered in his bed with his hands chopped off, private parts removed and stuffed in his mouth, the dead bird at his side. The boyfriend was never seen again.

I was with my attorney Ron in Los Angeles when the phone rang. Ron picked up the phone ... "Yes I can hear you quite well. Who is this?" It was the boyfriend. He was pleading for Ron's help. He claimed that he had returned to Rancho Cuernavaca to claim a leather coat that he had left and the authorities nabbed him. " ... wait ... wait ... You're breaking up ... I'm going under a bridge ..." Ron hung up the phone, looked at me and said, "Oops, I forgot I was on a landline!"

CHAPTER 14

Do You Know Who I Could Have Been?

I always believed that I was destined to be a star. As a very young boy, I went searching for a piano at every gathering ... whenever I found it and played a considerable audience would assemble to see the adorable prodigy. Everything came easy to me. As I entered adulthood, my adventurous personality deterred me from the path to greatness. Despite the challenges I rediscovered my sense of direction, but ... *Do You Know Who I Could Have Been?*

I Don't Have a Drinking Problem

People with addictions are always in denial. Obese overeaters insist, "I'm not fat, I'm just big-boned." Compulsive gamblers run out of excuses for unaccounted time and always being broke. Sex addicts usually do their best work in the church basement. I never thought I was an alcoholic; I just drank a lot, and not all the time. My drinking ran a pattern. I would start off with an evening of cocktails and dinner. The following morning a single shot of vodka would ease the pain. Then onto a liquid lunch that continued into the night until "last call." By the third day I was in my cups, secretly swigging straight from the bottle at my bar and chasing it with Coca-Cola. I would lock the doors and refused to answer the phone. I often found receipts yet had no recollection of where I had been the night before; a nine hundred dollar limousine bill and a pricey dinner at Escoffier did not deter me from continuing the pattern.

I woke up one morning in a tuxedo sleeping outside my apartment door. I had no keys and my car was missing. A neighbor exited next door and reminded me that I told him of my plans to dine at LeDome the night before. I walked up the hill to LeDome where the management had taken my keys and put me in a cab. Another occasion I picked a guy up in a bar on Santa Monica Boulevard. I took him to my apartment and while I was passed out he robbed me and stole my car.

The scariest episode was when I was driving to Laguna Beach on the 405 freeway. I blacked out as I was passing the exit for LAX and came to an hour later when I arrived at my destination, still rolling.

I Gave Up Drinking for Drugs

I was having lunch at the Bistro Garden in Beverly Hills with the kingpin of the Columbian mafia when he handed me a vile of cocaine under the table. He called it the "One Hundred-Dollar-a-Day Beverly Hills Diet." Cocaine never really did it for me, but after moving to the desert I discovered that crystal meth did. It was cheap and easily available. My partner Johnny and I started whiffing and smoking and at first it was fun. It was a lot of fun. With a loss of inhibitions and increase in our sexual appetites we invited everyone in who wanted to party. Buff, beautiful boys were in the pool and Jacuzzi and filled every room in our house. Men came and went throughout the day and at all hours of the night.

The house was full of men one evening when a friend arrived from out-of-town. He parked his RV on the street and ran a ratty extension cord across the lawn tapping into an outlet near the front door. The meth pipe passed between everyone as they hurriedly partnered up to indulge in intimate activity. In the midst of the mad frenzy a breaker popped and the house went dark. The sprinklers in the front had kicked on and sparked the damaged extension cord. I stumbled over numerous naked bodies as I tried to locate an opening and get to the breaker box. The darkness did not disrupt the meth-fueled orgy. When the lights came back on all men were happily with somebody else!

Things started to get ugly. Clothing and jewelry began to disappear. We had to hide wallets, cash and credit cards. Roommates began to bring in unwanted vagrants who brought their friends in as well. Neighbors threatened to file complaints. The fatal blow hit when the police came to the front door asking for one of the roommates. They searched the wrong room and found nothing, but the suspect was arrested for personal possession. After the cops took him away we entered his locked room and found enough drugs to ship us all off to the big house. It stopped being fun.

I Want My Life Back

Johnny came into my office and sat down, both of us still reeling from the close call with the police. He said, "Do you realize how serious that could have been?" I did not. But when he started to explain that they could have seized the house, everything in it and us as well, I was profoundly aware that the party was over. Our addiction had consumed our lives for the previous five years. We had both kept our jobs and continued to work; however everything we made had gone up in smoke. Johnny said, "We gotta stop sometime." To which I responded, "I want to stop now," and Johnny agreed.

After Johnny left, I sat in silence and surveyed the room, taking in the sight of hundreds of autographed celebrity photos, numerous keys to cities and awards from my life before drugs. I saw how close I had come to losing it all, but it wasn't too late to reel it back in.

Recovery Is a Bitch

Just like that, we stopped. The boys in residence were very unhappy when together Johnny and I announced, "No more drugs in the house." And they quickly disappeared.

I kept myself occupied by cleaning and organizing the abandoned belongings of the roommates, which we then bagged and left them in the yard alongside the house. I did not want any of the guys back inside. Once the house was cleared of all debris we "Bible wiped" everything. In doing so we found forgotten bags of dope concealed beneath carpets, tucked under drawer liners, and taped in toilet tanks. We even discovered a baggie full of syringes in the garden.

Once the house was clean and drug-free we struggled to reassemble our lives, sleeping most of the day to be able to make it back to work at night. Motivation was at a low though our appetites began to return. After about a week we started to level out. The depression that follows drug cessation is overwhelming and the most daunting side effect of recovery. Our craving for meth continued for quite some time, but we were able to resist its attraction.

Removing Toxic People from My Life

An energy vampire is a good name for them; people who suck the life out of you. And you may not even be aware that it is happening. My friend John Peter Hagen, author of *Play Away Please*, told me that he barely has time to spend with the people he likes and he won't waste it on those he does not! This relevance is not limited to a particular group of people. *Family* ... The other F word! Some relatives are better loved from a distance. Friends who are negative and draining should not be counted as friends. Dump them on the roadside and drive on! Put someone in the passenger seat that will add some zing to your life. Drama! Who needs it? Not me!

During the eighteen months that I took care of my mother in Indianapolis, I learned a lot about the people who were around me. I discovered the people who were enhancing my life and those who were not. I recognized those who took for themselves and gave nothing in return. Some people constantly complain and put others down. They attempt to instill guilt and futilely criticize. They pop up like annoying pimples. Over time I learned to stay clear of them. One thing that they all have in common is an objective to leave us powerless, depleted, and vulnerable. The effects of their negativity can affect both physical health and mental state. My 2013 New Year's resolution was to surround myself with people and circumstances that enhanced my life.

On a flight from New York to Los Angeles in 2009, I read an unforgettable quote from a celebrity interview with Johnny Depp. *Vanity Fair* said, "He's remarkably averse to conflict, pruning the toxic people from his life." Another quote that's helped me this year is a poem from an anonymous author:

When you leave certain people, do you feel better or feel worse?
Which ones always have drama or don't really understand, know and
appreciate you and the gift that lies within you?
Everyone can't be in Your FRONT ROW.

The more you seek God and the things of God, the more you seek quality, the
more you seek not just the hand of God but the face of God, the more you
seek things honorable, the more you seek growth, peace of mind, love and
truth around you, the easier it will become for you to decide who gets to sit in
the FRONT ROW and who should be moved to the balcony of your life.
Everyone can't be in Your FRONT ROW.

You cannot change the people around you ... but you can change
the people you are around!
Ask God for wisdom and discernment and choose wisely the people
who sit in the FRONT ROW of your life.

Remember that FRONT ROW seats are for special and deserving people and
those who sit in your FRONT ROW should be chosen carefully.
Everyone Can't be in Your FRONT ROW.

CHAPTER 15

Life's a Bitch, and So Are You!

Now and then we all meet someone who is impossible to deal with. *Agatha Trunchbull. Cruella de Vil.* There's not enough time to spend with the people I like, much less waste time on those that I loathe! *Elvira Gulch. Mrs. Drysdale.* What makes some people think they are entitled? *Miranda Priestly. Baby Jane Hudson.* Life is invaluable. It doesn't always treat us fairly. Who needs bitches? We all do! It's healthy! Can't live with 'em, Can't live with 'em! It gives me the greatest of pleasure to introduce you to some of the evil people in my life and say something that is long overdue … *Life's a Bitch, and So Are You!*

Says Who?

Mr. Blackwell liked me, but I did not like him. He insulted everyone around him as much as possible. He fancied himself a fashion designer but was more of a has-been that never was. As a columnist he was more of a who's-not than a who's-who. Any fag could pick out the worst dressed women in America.

Blackwell gave me a scathing review in the *Beverly Hills Courier*. He reviewed me with his cutthroat point of view and disrespected me. But when I saw him he told me, "Your problem is that you get better looking and more talented all of the time."

"Then why the bad review?" I asked.

He confessed, "I never put truth in print."

Gabored To Tears

I was just nine years old when the American sitcom *Green Acres* initially aired on CBS in 1965. I found the premise of the show to be exceedingly frustrating. Oliver Wendell Douglas' (Eddie Albert) nonsensical ambition to be a farmer was absurd enough on it's own. But plucking Lisa (Eva Gabor), his glamorous wife, from her Park Avenue penthouse and dragging her to Hooterville was, even from my adolescent point of view, ludicrously intolerable! I yearned to see her, diamond-bedecked, floating from one elegant room to the next of a lofty apartment in abundant pastel chiffon and feathers. A shabby lean-to just didn't cut it for me! And I never dreamed that I would someday meet that gorgeous creature in person.

Dino Gigante introduced me to Eva Gabor at the Bill Palmer Salon in the Beverly Hills Hotel in 1980. Dino was a well-known coiffeur to the stars and although Eva was not his client, he was familiar enough with her to make the introduction. During the early '80s, the Bill Palmer Salon was a notably popular spot for celebrities and socialites who habitually chased magnificence. It wasn't unusual to see Joan Collins, Audrey Meadows, or Anne Miller luxuriating in sartorial splendor.

On that consecrated afternoon, Dino reverently led me into a private treatment room where Miss Gabor was quietly reclining. I was shocked to find her with hair in foil, wearing a lime green facial mask. Dino whispered her name, and she opened her eyes. When she gathered her senses, she gave a slight smile and greeted us with the distinctive Hungarian Gabor parlance. Somewhere in the short-lived but very gracious exchange, I mustered enough nerve to ask what I, a Hollywood newcomer, should do to launch my career.

Gesturing with a jeweled hand, she said, "Start at the bottom and work your way to the top, dahling!" Then she smiled and returned to the reclining position and shut her eyes.

That very same afternoon, I was puttering along on Sunset Boulevard in my little white hatchback Dodge Omni when a gleaming black Rolls Royce Corniche convertible caught my eye. The California license plate boldly stated "ZZZZZ"! When I pulled alongside at a traffic light, I beeped my anemic horn to get the driver's attention while emphatically pointing to the back right wheel of the car.

The tinted window lowered, and here came, once again, that distinctive Hungarian Gabor parlance as the driver questioned, "Vhat is it dahling?" Who would imagine I would meet two Gabors within one hour. I shouted back, "Your wheel cover is loose!" When the light turned green, Zsa Zsa pulled to the curb and stopped, and I pulled in directly behind her. I leapt out of my vehicle and dropped to the ground, planted my posterior on the hot street, and kicked the wheel cover with my heels into a secure snap-fit position. I then jumped to my feet and eagerly approached the driver's window to tell Zsa Zsa the ironic tale of just having met her sister.

Once again, a gesturing jeweled hand appeared, giving an apathetic wave as she sped away announcing over her shoulder that she was en route to the airport and was running late.

The Rolls swiftly merged into the stream of traffic and was gone.

I stood at the edge of Sunset Boulevard and smiled. She was heading in the opposite direction of the airport.

Zsa Zsa was a regular at Jimmy's, Chasen's, the Bistro, and the Bistro Garden in Beverly Hills. I would see her at the annual holiday party at the Kasteel Kamphuyzen, where host Herbert Hischemoeller often solicited me to assist him in keeping Zsa Zsa a safe distance from the Christmas tree. Two powder-wigged sentries stood at attention throughout the evening next to the tree to ensure that the real candles with very real flames did not catch fire to anything, particularly Zsa Zsa's ball gown.

In 1988, Nolan Miller, famed Dynasty costume designer, graciously asked me to slip behind the baby grand for his couture fashion show and cocktail reception at the Four Seasons Hotel in Beverly Hills. He also made travel arrangements for my mother to fly in for the glamorous event. Elizabeth Taylor, Angie Dickinson, Linda Evans, and Stephanie Beacham were among the guests.

Nolan chose to avoid the media madness by standing with Mom and me near the piano as the celebrities arrived. Zsa Zsa, wearing a crimson ball gown, made a flamboyant entrance. As she floated across the room, Nolan put his arm around Mom's waist and corralled her toward the piano and closer to me. He leaned in and pointed out the plethora of plush ruffles that generously flowed from the shoulders of the gown. His eyes sparkled when he said in a stage whisper, "I did that to hide her fat ass!" Mom blushed and smiled.

In September of 1989, I happened upon Princess Zsa Zsa standing in the checkout queue at Pavilions Market in West Hollywood. She was with her ninth husband, Germany's Prince Frederick von Anhalt, Duke of Saxony. With typical arrogance she snapped at the gawking shoppers, "Well, we need to eat too?" One week later she was arrested for slapping a police officer in Beverly Hills. My good friend Ronald Jason Palmieri defended her in the case. Then Zsa Zsa lost a lengthy feud with actress Elke Sommer in a Los Angeles court battle in 1993. Sommer was awarded $3.3 million in damages from Gabor and Prince Freddy for defamation of character. It seems that Zsa Zsa just couldn't help rearing her ugly head in those days. It is rumored that the infamous couple never did cough up the bucks.

Interestingly enough, the Gabors never really excelled at anything in particular. Socialite, Elsa Maxwell claimed that they were simply "famous for being famous." Much like the Kardashians, Matriarch Mama Jolie encouraged her three exquisite progenies with the inspiration that they would be famous, rich, and marry kings. And marry they did indeed! As they moved about and modified their lifestyles, they collectively sashayed through twenty-three matrimonial moments between the four of them.

It was not until I moved to Palm Springs in 1996 that I became better acquainted with them and aware of their forty-year legacy in the desert.

For a number of years, Zsa Zsa purportedly "owned" a table just inside the entrance of the Bamboo Lounge at the famed Racquet Club in Palm Springs. Table 8, like her Palm Springs home, was sheathed in red. Red tablecloth, flowers, and linens were in place for her at all times. Her loyalty to the club ended on one particular evening when she arrived unannounced to find that her table had been surrendered to an unfamiliar party. She stormed out of the Racquet Club and never returned.

The five-star French restaurant, Le Vallauris, became Zsa Zsa's new preferred dining venue. Owner Paul Bruggeman was a classic Belgian-Franco gentleman who possessed the innate ability to accommodate the most discerning international connoisseurs of fine dining. When Paul's beloved mother passed away, multitudes of friends and patrons gathered at Our Lady of Solitude Catholic Church in Palm Springs to pay final respects and attend the mass. My good friend Teena and I arrived quite early to avoid the crowd and secure a sensible spot. The multitudes began to appear and steadily fill the church. Suddenly, there was a commotion at the rear of the church. The Gabors had arrived—all four of them, decked in brightly colored couture costumes, dramatic picture hats, and coordinated gloves. They ambled down the center aisle, grabbing the attention of the entire turnout, and slid into the pew directly in front of us. The wall of broad bills and brims completely blocked our view of the front of the church, and by the time the fabulous four had settled in, there were no seats left for us to move to. So we listened to the mass and were granted a peek only when one of the hats shifted during a prayer, sneeze, or sniffle.

In 1994 Bruggeman invited me to slip behind the baby grand at his Le Vallauris lounge, where I became more familiar with the Gabor girls. Jolie was well into her nineties, and being quite frail, she rarely ventured out. Magda, the eldest sister, now in a wheelchair, was still glamorous, elegant, and engaging. Zsa Zsa entertained in small numbers typically on someone else's tab. Eva was by far the most pleasant of the tribe. The first time I saw her at Le Vallauris, I mentioned our introduction at the hair salon many years prior. She graciously acknowledged recalling the event and was more than sweet to do so as I knew she had no idea of what I was talking about. Eva was prettiest of the four. She frequently arrived on the arm of Merv Griffin for dinners and special events.

The news of Eva's death on July 4, 1995, was shocking. She reportedly succumbed to respiratory failure and pneumonia at Cedars-Sinai Hospital in Los Angeles, though it was rumored that her death was a fault of the hospital. Some say that she fell in the bathtub while on holiday at her vacation home in Mexico. Others said it was on the stairs. Whatever the case, I was greatly saddened by her passing. She was only seventy-four, the youngest of the brood.

On the day of the funeral, I made a morning phone call to my diva girlfriend, Sharon Stanley, to see if she would accompany me and my then-partner Stefan Ebert to the funeral at the Church of the Good Shepherd in Beverly Hills.

Stefan and I wore dark suits. Sharon was turned out in a smart black Chanel dress, gloves, Jackie O shades, and a veiled picture hat the size of a Walgreen's. As we approached the entrance to the church, we were halted by security who searched for our names on the guest list—where, I knew, they were not. I kicked into stage-mode and delivered a convincing narrative that eventually granted us entry. At the close of the service, we contentedly remained seated in the back of the church and watched Nancy Reagan, Eddie Albert, Merv Griffin, Johnny Mathis, and many others make their way out of the church and into the barrage of the fervent paparazzi and a procession of limousines parked halfway around the block. It was a very sad but memorable occasion.

On September 29 of that year, I was asked to perform for Jolie's ninety-ninth birthday at Le Vallauris. It was like a classic scene from a Fellini movie. The guests ranged in age from ninety to Forest Lawn. Some needed to be propped up and balanced in armchairs.

Zsa Zsa did not attend, and in the wake of Eva's passing, a somewhat somber mood prevailed. When the party ended, I volunteered to help Jolie out to her waiting Rolls near the front door. It was an awkward venture. To securely hold onto her elbow and forearm with both hands, I had to lean to the left to avoid the brim of her hat. When I finally plunked her into the front seat, she insisted that I kiss her goodbye. Leaning in, I had to contort my body so that I could steer clear of that hat and find her face. With surprising strength, she shot both hands up, gripped my head and heaved me into the car. I lost my balance and fell into her as our faces collided. When I was able to finally gain my balance, I bid her farewell, shut the door and the car rolled away. It wasn't until sometime later on a visit to the men's room when I discovered Jolie's freshly applied red lipstick was smeared across my right cheek. That was some kiss!

Jolie passed away on April 1, 1997, in Palm Springs. Magda followed two months later on June 6. Zsa Zsa is now ninety-six and recently sold her Bel Air home for $11 million. She and her husband are allowed to remain in the mansion until she dies.

It was a rare treat to be so close to living legends. The combination of timeless beauty, celebrated legacy, and spontaneous radiance is rare. The opportunity to experience it was remarkable!

I Sleep Alone

I met Rip Taylor at the home of director Ross Hunter. Rip hit on me seconds before we were introduced. He was a control freak. As he gave me his phone number he ordered that we synchronize our watches. I was to call his hotel room at precisely 11:04 the following morning. A minute before or after, he would not take the call. I followed his precise orders and was given a plane ticket to fly to Las Vegas. When I arrived in Vegas he dragged me through hotels and casinos, showing me off as his arm candy. Later that evening, we finally returned to his house. When we retired for the night he said, "You can sleep in there … Or in here." I slept in there.

During my engagement with Liberace, my reviews far outshined Rip's. So when I sent him a Christmas letter, he returned it with a handwritten note on the back, "You are as warm in printed page as you attempt to be humble." He has avoided me ever since!

Have Any Other Boring Stories to Share?

In the 1980s, Grace and Harold Robbins sold their house in Beverly Hills; the Villa Grazia in the south of France; and their yacht, *Gracara*, to settle in an upscale Palm Springs neighborhood. The Las Palmas house paled in comparison to those of neighboring residents Kirk Douglas and Sidney Sheldon. The property consisted of the main house and three guesthouses, one of which Harold used as his office and private space.

One day Grace asked if I would drive her back to Palm Springs after a social weekend in Los Angeles. When we arrived we were pleased to find Harold in an unusually pleasant mood. He invited me to join them for dinner, which turned out to be a dismal event.

Harold was seated at the head of the long dining table with Grace and me at either side. As the maid served dinner, I sensed the tension between Harold and Grace and struggled to initiate a conversation. Against a backdrop of uneasy silence, I rattled off what I considered an interesting story. To impress the best-selling author, I chose my words carefully and was deliberate in my phrasing and delivery. As the suspense developed, and my excitement elevated, I completed the story with a dynamic finish. Boom!

Following a moment of demoralizing silence Harold growled, "Do you have any other boring stories to share with us?" I was shocked. Fuck him!

About a month later, my mother was visiting when we made the trip out to Palm Springs. One of the first things she wanted to do was meet the famous Harold Robbins. I reluctantly phoned Grace to see if we might be able to stop by. Before making the call, I prayed she would not invite us to dinner. My prayers were answered.

We arrived early afternoon and Grace escorted us to Harold's lair. When we stepped in, Harold looked like E.T. phoning home. Following a short introduction, I asked him if I could take a picture of them together. Mom made her way around the desk to stand next to Harold in his wheelchair.

"On three ... One, two, three ..." The camera captured a contorted expression on my mother's face, but intimidation prevented me from asking for another shot.

"What was with the face?" I asked her after we'd left.

"He grabbed my backside!"

Knocking me out at dinner was enough, but grabbing my mom's ass had just done me in!

Zelda Rubinstein

One of the more frightening scenes in a movie (that disturbs me to this day) was in Steven Spielberg's 1982 horror film, *Poltergeist*. Two terrified children huddle together in their bedroom and count the lessening lapsing seconds between lightening strikes and claps of thunder of an approaching thunderstorm. As the storm intensifies, Carol Anne's big brother focuses on a creepy gnarled backyard tree. With a flash and a crash, the tree suddenly becomes animated and grabs Robbie through the bedroom window as his little sister is sucked through a portal in the closet. In the course of the plot, a squat, quirky medium, played by Zelda Rubinstein, is introduced and successfully "cleans" the spiritual presence from the family's house.

A personal introduction to Zelda Rubinstein in the spring of 1985 was equally as frightening as the movie! In person, she was toad-like in appearance. She couldn't be troubled with autographs or pictures. She was snippy, sarcastic and audaciously demanding. It's doubtful that when that bitch crossed over it was into the light.

CHAPTER 16

We'll Leave the Light On

As a child, I always anticipated holiday breaks from school and summer vacation. After seemingly infinite amounts of time pouring over roadmaps, Dad would check the timers attached to lamps in tactical locations throughout the house while Mom vacuumed the living room carpet one last time. My brother was in charge of arranging suitcases, coolers filled with cold drinks and bags filled with every imaginable snack. I focused on collecting the necessary stuffed animals that always escorted me on every journey. When all preparations were complete, we would collectively pile into the family station wagon and roll. Dad would stop the car at the end of the driveway for a brief but very sincere prayer of thanks for the opportunity to travel and to bring us safely home.

Those were cherished times. A simple lodging with neon lights, advertising air-conditioning, TVs and a swimming pool. The characteristic aroma of a motel room somewhere miles from home. Through the years I have had some wonderful experiences and met some most-amazing people in hotels, motels, and bed and breakfasts around the world. Follow me to the Bel Age Hotel in West Hollywood, where I met more famous folk during my engagement there than any other given time in my life. Follow me to where I flourished at the Steinway grand in the celebrated lounge, and I promise … *We'll Leave the Light On.*

Bette Davis

It was a busy Saturday night. The piano lounge was energized with a blissful and glamorous cast of characters. Many of my faithful followers were in attendance. Comfy sectional sofas filled the corners that flanked the Steinway grand piano. From the piano bench, I had a commanding view of the bar that ran the length the room. Good friends Bob and Cindy sat in the sectional to my right, so that she could monitor the room's activities. I was wholeheartedly ensconced in one of my tales when I noticed Cindy staring over my left shoulder. I turned and saw a flock of flawless young men seated to my left. In the middle of an abundant pack of captivating manliness was a coiffed, jeweled, and equally captivating Bette Davis. I continued to play as I watched our esteemed visitor.

I was not aware until recently that Bob and Cindy followed Bette Davis to her house that night. Once Miss Davis had gone inside, they knocked on her front door. Cindy just so happened to have one of Bette Davis' books in the car that she wanted to have autographed. Bette answered the door, autographed the book, and sent them on their way. It's a wonder that they weren't arrested.

Christopher Plummer

It's amazing how quickly some people bond, especially over a cocktail and a soft playing piano. Christopher Plummer is one of the more dapper gentlemen in the film industry. I can remember going to see *The Sound of Music* as a child and sensing the strength of his character. What a classically handsome man. I never imagined that some years later, I would have the opportunity to sit and chat with the legendary actor.

Mr. Plummer stayed in the Bel Age Hotel for about six weeks in the mid-80s, during which time he frequented the piano lounge, mostly during the cocktail hour following a day of filming on location. He usually sat quietly at the bar, paying no attention to anything that went on around him. In the one conversation that I did have with him we discussed the filming of *The Sound of Music*. After the filming concluded, Christopher Plummer remained in Europe for almost a year. Upon his return to the states, he was astounded to find that the film was a smash hit. He could get any table at any restaurant … anywhere … anytime. He always said, "I discovered the true meaning of being a celebrity."

Prince

In 1985, *Purple Rain* won an Academy Award for Best Music, Original Song Score. I salivated over the purple-sequined hooded cloak that Prince wore on the night that he accepted the award. I was not aware that he was staying in the Bel Age Hotel until I was nearly run down in the car park by his chauffeur-driven purple Cadillac limo. Prince emerged from the vehicle surrounded by giant bodyguards who bulldozed through the crowd to make way for the newly celebrated pop icon.

I later learned that he had become notorious for causing a scene wherever he appeared—it was about the same time that he altered his title, asserting that he would be henceforth known as The Artist Formerly Known as Prince, and he would not attend the award ceremony unless he could be accommodated to have no one sit in front, behind or to either side of him. His wish was not granted; however, he did attend.

While staying in the hotel, he brought an entourage of personal stylists, attendants, and chefs. Another demand was to have exclusive use of the Alex Roldan Salon on the main floor of the hotel. The floor to ceiling glass windows where draped with white sheets, so that passers by could not peer in from the hallway.

One night he strolled into the lounge in a white sailor's uniform with matching eight-inch patent leather platformed shoes and an oversized captains hat. He posed, made a brief scan of the crowd, and then vanished. What a putz!

Christopher Reeve

Why do gay guys insist that every handsome man is gay? Sorry fellas, Christopher Reeve was straight ... completely and totally. During his six-week stay at the Bel Age Hotel, Christopher Reeve visited the lounge at the same hour every afternoon and sat at the same bar stool; third from the wall, on the corner. After seating, he would acknowledge me with a nod and a smile. The mere sight of him made me lightheaded, and I had to struggle to keep my focus on the keys. When we met, I immediately hit on him, "Would your wife mind if we went out for dinner?" He replied, "Dinner's fine, but no dessert."

David Bowie

Before I met him, I thought of David Bowie as Ziggy Stardust, an androgynous nonconformist-rocker sporting psychedelic face paint and flaming mullet-mop of hair. Eccentricity is not an unfamiliar characteristic in British culture. The one obsession that definitely weaves a prominent thread throughout the Empire is the profound fondness of tea. Tea is the breath of life and that is exactly where I met David Bowie, breathing in the aroma of a cup of Darjeeling brew in the calm corner of my piano lounge on a quiet afternoon. Alone, tranquil, and pensive, he sat. I approached and introduced myself. He was pleasant but forthright, informing me that he was carrying out a ritual of meditation prior to a concert that evening. I left him without more ado and as I walked away I found myself amazed at how, in an instant, the megastar transformed from a rowdy rebellious rocker to a refined English gentleman.

Tommy Tune

I met Tommy Tune in the lobby of the Bel Age hotel. I was entering from the valet parking when I spotted all six-feet-six-inches of him standing at the reception desk. The most distinguishing part of him was his gargantuan bright turquoise ostrich-skin cowboy boots. They looked like river barges. So I marched right up, introduced myself and asked him, "How the hell do you dance in those things?"

His simple response was, "Very well."

Oprah Winfrey

In the mid-'80s Oprah's show became a national sensation. She was in Los Angeles and stopped by the Bel Age during a quiet cocktail hour. Oprah was wearing a periwinkle suit with black piping (only a fag would take notice of that!). She sat on a banquet next to the piano and began shuffling through a briefcase. Oprah looked at me, smiled and said, "Is there anyplace I can get a breath mint? The kiosk is closed."

Shielding her mouth with her hand she added, "I had garlic for lunch."

I wondered for a moment why the dining room didn't have dinner mints, then reached inside the piano for a pack of gum offering her a piece. "I have gum."

She hesitated. I was unaware then that Oprah Winfrey has a gum phobia. She is completely anti-gum and even banned the stuff from her building. She firmly said, "I don't chew gum, but I need it."

She took a piece, unwrapped it, popped it into her mouth, and gave it a few chomps. Oprah turned and looked to her left and saw three people entering, "Here's my appointment." She took the gum from her mouth, dropped it and exclaimed, "Oh … I lost it!" She stood up, turned full circle, "Do you see it? Is it stuck to my skirt?" It was not. She picked up her briefcase and nodded to me as she walked away with the group. I quickly searched the banquet area and found the lost gum and mashed it onto a page in the guest book. I covered it with cellophane and wrote, "Oprah Winfrey's Chewed Chewing Gum." I still have the gum. Just think … I have Oprah Winfrey's DNA!

CHAPTER 17

Famous Faux Pas

Everyone on the planet has survived a modicum of embarrassing moments, be it at their own expense or that of someone else's. There are those "open mouth, insert both feet" circumstances that provoke a crowd to glow with red faces. Even if some instances cause horrendous discomfort, they many times become terribly amusing in retrospect. I love to laugh and I hope you will laugh with me as I share with you some of my most memorable … *Famous Faux Pas.*

The Imposter

In the mid-eighties I was hosting a show at the Rose Tattoo in West Hollywood. *Star in Pursuit* ran for forty-six weeks every Sunday. Five boys and five girls competed each week in vocal competition. There were four rotating judges that sat in a panel in front of the stage, often I would choose celebrities to bring fame to the show. Paul Lynde, Zelda Rubenstien, Rosalind Kind, and Shelley Winters were among some of the celebrated names.

During the time the show was running, an attractive young man in his twenties surfaced in the West Hollywood society scene. He came to the show one night, introducing himself as Harry Belafonte's son Deroy. Tall, slender, and graceful, the resemblance to his father was striking! His cocoa complexion and sultry eyes with that captivating stare melted me. When Deroy Belafonte spoke I could not distinguish his voice from his father's. Deroy expressed an interest in joining the competition; however, being a celebrity's son I felt that with his looks, voice, and noted name he would be unfair competition to the others. When I suggested he serve as a celebrity judge instead, he lit up. The following Sunday, Deroy joined the panel of distinguished judges including Dick Sargent as well as the owners of the club.

After the show, a group of us gathered at my apartment for a party that ran until morning. The crowd dispersed at about 4:00 a.m. Later that morning, I received a phone call from my friend Phillip Buck. After a night of wild abandon, Phillip and Deroy had made it to the Beverly Hills Hotel for breakfast. Phillip lit up a cigarette while waiting for Deroy to return to the car. When he opened the ashtray of Deroy's BMW, he was surprised to find a stash of my then-partner Dale Brunner's jewelry. While in Vegas I had several pieces of jewelry designed with Dale's initials: a ring, a bracelet, and a pendant on a gold chain. They were emblazed with diamond initials DB. Dale Brunner. Deroy Belafonte. The similarity was uncanny. You see, when I brought Deroy home for the party, and I gave him the privacy to shower and change, I never suspected that he would ransack my room and help himself to my partner's jewelry!

My first reaction was to call the West Hollywood Sheriff. A deputy arrived at the apartment and advised me to contact Deroy Belafonte and somehow lure him back to my apartment. I got Deroy back to the apartment with an invitation for vocal rehearsals. How he loved to sing—so much so that he returned within the hour. Perhaps the real draw was his wanting to return for drinks and another line of cocaine.

Just before Deroy's arrival, the deputy stepped around the corner into the dining room. Deroy entered the apartment, and before turning over the music I hit him point-blank.

"Apparently you have some of my jewelry, and I would like to have it back."

I was shocked when he shot back: "I don't have it anymore. I already hocked it."

At that very moment the deputy appeared from around the corner, with a look of utter disbelief on his face. He read Deroy his rights and cuffed him.

Once I got over the shock, I decided to seize the opportunity to share my story with the world, and see if I could make a buck. I called the *National Enquirer*. "Son of Celebrity Arrested in West Hollywood Apartment."

But someone beat me to it! I never expected my call to be directed to Barbara Sternig, senior reporter for the tabloid, who told me that the West Hollywood Sheriff had already contacted her. She also informed me that Harry Belafonte had no son named Deroy, his kids were Shari and David. Not only was Deroy Belafonte an impostor, he didn't even exist. His real name was Deroy Greene. He had been bedding everyone and anyone in West Hollywood under the guise of his celebrity, and while they slumbered, spent from the pleasures of Deroy's flesh, he helped himself to their baubles and bankroll. In exchange for their valuables, he was also sharing something of his own. He was riddled with venereal disease. Fortunately I never made it between the sheets with him.

Nice Chord Change

Everybody wants to steal the limelight. Just because a microphone is present doesn't mean that you get to use it. Why is it when people see a piano they insist on to playing it? My two pet peeves: Don't touch a keyboard when I am playing it, and don't even think of helping yourself to one of my McDonald's French fries!

During cocktail hour at the Excelsior on Rodeo Drive, a relatively distinguished gentleman approached the grand piano just as I was completing a flamboyant rendition of a favorite Tony Bennett song, "A Time for Love." He stood patiently to my right, and when I finished he unabashedly volunteered that he had an alternate chord change that was significant to the song. He sat down on the bench and slid me off to the left as he commandeered the keyboard. How rude! But he was right. The single chord change altered the phrasing of the entire song. He segued into another tune and continued to play with inimitable style that captivated the audience. I was equally impressed with his performance and annoyed by his audacity.

When the applause waned, I congratulated him and introduced myself, "That was wonderful. I'm Jere Ring."

He smiled, shook my hand and said, "Thanks. I'm André Previn."

I'm Falling Out Of My Dress

On February 28, 1986, I was invited to attend a concert featuring Barbara Mandrell at the then-Universal Amphitheatre in Los Angeles. It was the famed Country music singer's first appearance since her miraculous recovery from a serious automobile accident on September 11, 1984. Along with a broken right leg and ankle, a damaged right knee, and various cuts and bruises, Barbara's head injury was so severe that she suffered temporary memory loss. It took well over two years for her to recuperate enough to perform again—and perform she did indeed! Miss Mandrell's publicist and I had become friendly while she was staying at the Bel Age Hotel where I performed. When she mentioned the concert, I expressed an interest and she issued an invitation and arranged for Dale Brunner (my "partner") and me to be picked up by Kenny Roger's limousine and transported to the Amphitheatre. The limo was great but unfortunately, it was Kennyless. He had cancelled at the last minute.

When we arrived at the Amphitheatre, we found ourselves in a long queue of limos. Once we arrived under the marquis, we emerged from our vehicle into a barrage of camera flashes aimed at Steve Allen and Jayne Meadows as they climbed out of the car in front of ours. A group of teenagers popped out of the car behind us and fell into the procession in sequence. As we entered the building, I turned to a cute young blond guy and spoke and just as the words, "I know you from somewhere" left my lips, I could feel my face redden with embarrassment.

"Ricky Schroeder," he said as he smiled and presented his hand to shake mine. He looked just like he did on TV. But at the age of sixteen there was very little if any need at all for makeup.

The then-Universal Amphitheatre is tremendous, seating over 6,000. We had great seats, seven rows from the front and slightly to the left of the stage. I recognized quite a few familiar famous faces as we were escorted through security and directed to our seats. Once we arrived at our row, I slipped in and seated myself in the second seat. Dale took the aisle. After settling in, I turned and introduced myself to the woman sitting next to me, "Hi. I'm Jere Ring, and this is Dale Brunner." She responded with a Nashville twang, "Hi. I'm Tammy Wynette. This is my husband, George." I was stunned, surprised and pleased. But as I looked beyond Tammy and her husband, just down the aisle I spotted Florence Henderson seated with Dolly Parton and her husband Carl Thomas.

The Barbara Mandrell Show was outstanding. At intermission I was shocked when good friends Bob and Cindy Mills showed up unexpectedly in the aisle. I asked them, "When did they start admitting peasants to the VIP section?!" Handing the camera to Cindy, as Tammy and I posed for the picture Tammy gritted her teeth and said, "I think I am falling out of my dress." After the photo op, Tammy tucked her boob back in and we enjoyed the rest of the show.

Never Talk with Your Feet in Your Mouth

Toni Holt invited me to a New Year's Eve party in the late 1980s. One of the celebrities in attendance was Debbie Reynolds. I was seated at the main table with Toni to my left and Miss Reynolds directly across from me. We had never met. I nervously made it through the appetizer and salad without misfortune; however, when the main course arrived I just had to open my mouth. I directed a sincere compliment to Debbie: "I thoroughly enjoyed you in Music Man."

The table was dead silent. Toni patted my hand and leaned over to sweetly whisper in my ear, "That was Shirley Jones, dear …"

Where Do You Want the Blinds Hung?

Bob and Cindy, and a small group of friends gathered in front of the piano at Jimmy's in Beverly Hills. As always, the room was abuzz with excitement. I was taking the usual requests, belting out my typical showstoppers, and, after an hour of nonstop music, I decided to take a break and make the rounds, working the room. Amused with myself, I was in a joke-telling mood and wanted to drop a couple new ones. I floated back to my familiar group at the piano and pulled a new one out of the air.

"A woman was nude sunbathing by her pool at a home in Beverly Hills. The maid approached her and announced that the blind man was at the door. The nude woman responded, 'Let him in. He can't see me.' Upon entering the man said, 'Nice tits! Where do you want your blinds hung?'"

That is when Cindy introduced me to their guest. "Say hello to Lula Mae Hardaway"—Stevie Wonder's mother. I sheepishly smiled and returned to the piano thinking, *There will be no more blind jokes tonight.*

Want Your Teeth Back Now?

In the early '80s, Martha Raye frequented The Main Street, a little gay bar in Laguna Beach where I was performing. She used to gallivant with a wealthy old queen named Sidney Anderson, a notorious alcoholic. They would sit in the corner of the bar and sniff amyl nitrate. The combination of alcohol and poppers drove them into maddening episodes of hysterical laughter. On occasion, Martha Raye would approach the piano, always with drink in hand she would remove her false teeth, drop them in the vodka rocks and warble an off-key rendition of "Little Girl Blue." The crowd's reaction was one of both amusement and dismay. They didn't know what to think of her and neither did I.

Years later, when I was performing at Jimmy's in Beverly Hills, Martha came in with her new husband, Mark Harris, and a group of twenty people. She proceeded to get inebriated. And rather than take her out a convenient side-door to the restaurant, Mark looped his arms under hers from behind her and dragged her through the crowded restaurant and out the front door to the waiting limousine. By the time they reached the car, her bare heels were bleeding. Shame on you, Mark. In my opinion, you were Martha's greatest faux pas.

I Can't See With Your Tits In My Face

The Bel Age Hotel piano lounge was buzzing in 1985. James Brown came in with his entourage for his birthday celebration. The group of some twenty-odd people caused immediate chaos, when yet another group flooded in through the door. Tanya Tucker and a small clan of groupies were trashed and staggering. When the hotel manager appeared, I motioned him over to the piano to ask how to handle the escalating situation. He shared with me that they were VIPs and that he would "monitor" the situation. Tanya was a drunken mess! Her hair was in every direction, and makeup running the other way.

As the confusion mounted, James Brown came to the piano, sliding in and literally shoving me off of the bench. After he sang a more-than-pathetic rendition of "Happy Birthday" to himself, I managed to regain my position on the piano bench.

Then Tanya Tucker decided that she was going to outdo James. She told me to "play happy birthday" because she was going to sing … from my lap! With one foot on the piano bench, she grabbed my hair and flung the other leg over me, planting the other foot on the bench with her cookie in my face and then dropped onto my lap like a cinder block. I managed to find the keyboard with my hands and began to play "Happy Birthday."

"Why aren't you singing?" Tanya slurred.

I barked, "Get your tits outta my face and I will!" The room went silent. Cricket. Cricket.

Were Ya Born in a Barn?

In 1988, I hosted a fundraising concert for United Cerebral Palsy at the MGM Filmland in Los Angeles. My friend Nolan Miller, fashion designer to the stars, was kind enough to connect me with some of his celebrity clients. He would make a phone call and clear the way for me to personally deliver an invitation to them. Joanna Carson was among the group of celebrity invitations. A week before the concert, I drove to the Carson house in Bel Air. She and Johnny had separated at that point, and she was living in the house alone. When I arrived at the estate, the gates were open, so I drove into the motor court. When I parked, I noticed that the front door was wide open. I looked around for gardeners, possible pool man, anyone. With no one in sight, I decided to go on in. Once inside the living room, I was just about to give a "yoo-hoo," when Joanna Carson skitted across the room wearing nothing but a bra and panties. She stopped dead in her tracks, equally as surprised as I was. She ever so graciously asked, "May I help you?"

From the provocative tone of her voice, I wasn't quite sure where this was going, so I approached her and timidly handed her the invitation. She thanked me, and several days later I received a generous donation and a handwritten apology with regrets that she would be unable to attend the concert. I know that Nolan was her personal couture. I can only assume that her undergarments will remain Victoria's Secret.

Cork it!

The inaugural voyage of the SSC *Radisson Diamond* was not always smooth sailing. Invited guests enjoyed fabulous fare, open bar, and complimentary wines and champagnes of their choice. Robin Leach pompously paraded around the decks grabbing as much champagne and caviar as his paunchy little paws could carry. On the third night out he came into my piano lounge dressed in tattered tuxedo with a bottle of Dom Pérignon Rouge tucked under each arm and a tin of beluga caviar in each hand. He placed the pricey items on the piano and shouted, "Let's fucking party!"

With no provocation he opened one of the bottles, shook it up and showered my piano and me. Life styles of the rich and classless ...

The Big Yawn

The passenger manifest of a transatlantic crossing was typically peppered with seasoned travelers. For those who had a fear of flying it was their only option of getting to Europe. For yet others it was an annual holiday. I was playing the cocktail hour as we sailed out of South Hampton. A foursome settled at the table directly in front of me. A peculiar man with black-rimmed glasses and an ill-fitting red toupee was facing me. His face was grossly contorted whenever he spoke. As his eyes widened and he stretched his jaw, he looked at the ceiling and then down at the floor. There appeared to be something tragically wrong with this poor soul. Was the attractive blonde woman with him his sister? The old couple across from him surely had to be his parents. As soon as I could I took a break, I went to their table. I just had to know.

I introduced myself around the table beginning with the older couple. I then turned to the peculiar gent and offered my name. He returned, "I'm Arthur Ferrante and this is my wife Jena." I stepped back and thought, *Arthur Ferrante? Of the famed Ferrante and Teicher pianists? No way!* Mr. Ferrante continued, as he stretched his jaw and yawned, "You'll have to excuse me … We just flew over from … (yawn) … New York City … (stretch, yawn) … And my ears are stopped up."

CHAPTER 18

Rubbing Elbows

Opportunities present themselves in the guise of fashion. Celebrities are not always recognizable and may be standing unnoticeable right in front of you. Notable people are out among the common folk in ordinary situations everyday. They are among us when we eat, shop, and exercise and in the most unremarkable places. Keep your eyes and ears open. You may not know it when you are … *Rubbing Elbows!*

Things Go Better With Coke

Following Sammy Davis' closing night performance at Harrah's in Reno, he gave a party for a few close friends in the hotel penthouse. My choice of poison that night was rum and Coke. As the party began to fade the bartender excused himself, leaving us on our own. I joined Sammy behind the bar to mix one last drink. I opened the small refrigerator door to find it empty. Turning to Sammy I asked, "Is there any more Coke?"

He said, "Hold on a minute," and went into another room. He returned with what appeared to be a large saltshaker. Grabbing a silver tray from the bar, he unscrewed the lid and dumped its contents on the tray. He handed me a straw. I took a whiff, smiled and asked, "Now can I get some Coca-Cola?!"

We're Off to the Opera!

I was flattered when Ginger Rogers asked me to escort her to the performance of *Aida* in January of 1985. It was my first time at the opera in New York. What a way to go! Miss Rogers wore a floor-length beaded gown that was accented with a plethora of feathers across the shoulders. Shortly after I picked her up, her dress began molting. Throughout the performance, I was collecting the plumes and handing them to her. By the time we reached the reception, her handbag was overflowing with feathers. She said, "We should sell them for charity," and she began to hand them out to people as souvenirs.

One woman proudly displayed her feather between her fingers and said, "Look, I plucked this from Ginger Rogers!"

My Favorite Genius

Michael Feinstein was playing at the Toy Tiger in the San Fernando Valley when I first met him. He sent me a congratulatory telegram for my opening night with Liberace in Las Vegas. The night that I returned to Los Angeles, Michael came to my apartment and we cried together over the loss of his good friend Ira Gershwin. That was the only night that we came close to intimacy but we never made it to the bedroom. We became close friends instead.

He introduced me to the Excelsior on Rodeo Drive. On the night that the Excelsior closed, I went to Michael's show at the Mondrian Hotel on Sunset Boulevard and found him sitting alone at the piano in an empty room. We were both depressed. My venue had just closed while his was empty. He stopped playing as we sat together on the piano bench.

"I need to get away from performing," Michael confided. "Since you're not working now, maybe you would be interested in covering for me for two weeks. I'm going to record an album."

While Michael went into the studio to record *Pure Gershwin*, I kept his audience entertained. Due to my smashing two weeks at the Mondrian, I was asked to open up the Bel Age just down the street. During the next few years, Michael Feinstein and I had it sewn up on Sunset.

Since that time Michael and I have both enjoyed illustrious careers. The primary source of Michael's repertoire is based on *The Great American Songbook*. During a short backstage visit at one of his concerts, I told Michael that members of my audience frequently come to the piano and ask, "Do you do any of Michael Feinstein's music?" He suggested, "The next time they ask you, say, 'No. But he does plenty of mine!'"

Will You Marry Me ... Again?

On a typical Sunday afternoon in Los Angeles, famous comedian Jack Carter called me, and growled, "Jere, this is Jack Carter. You may not know Roxanne and I have been separated for eight years and we're gonna get married again. Will you play for the wedding?"

"Sure. When's the wedding?"

"Tuesday!"

Gee, thanks for the notice.

When I arrived at Iris Rothstein's plush penthouse, most of the guests had arrived. I went to the piano and began to play as the wedding party assembled. Holding the huppah were Don Rickles, Morey Amsterdam, Milton Berle, and Jan Murray. It was impossible for Jack and Roxanne to uphold the serenity of the moment. Rapid-fired jokes endlessly ricocheted around the room. Just as it seemed that the ceremony would never come to an end, Debbie Reynolds shouted, "Oh for Chrissake, step on the damn glass!" The rabbi gave the blessing and the most entertaining wedding I ever attended came to its end.

I Just Saw Her Last Night

Noted choreography and director Tony Charmoli held a spectacular annual holiday party. One year, Mom was my date and was pleased to meet Julie Andrews, Mitzi Gaynor and Cyd Charisse. When we had our picture taken with Shirley MacLaine, my brother said, "You'll probably get the photo back, and there will be you, Mom, and an empty space in between."

Mom was most excited when Linda Gray came through the front door and loudly exclaimed, "I just saw her last night!"

Puzzled, I asked, "Where?"

"On Dallas!"

The Incredible Mr. Limpet

Don Knotts loved my music. Whenever and wherever I was playing, he would show up … usually with a big-busted blonde. "I like my women tall." Bless his little heart, the women towered over him and that was the way he liked it. He once told me, "I would rather look up at 'em than bury my face in 'em."

Look into My Eyes

I only played for Elizabeth Taylor one time. When I arrived at her Bel Air home I mistakenly entered through the service door. I introduced myself to the staff and was taken to the grand piano in the living room. I started to play before the guests arrived. When I felt a gentle hand on my shoulder, I turned and gazed into her lavender eyes. "Hello, I'm Liz. Thank you for coming, you will be joining us for dinner." I played for a little more than an hour as the relatively dull guests arrived. None of them were recognizable. Larry Fortensky, her seventh husband, must have arranged the guest list. When dinner was finished I went in search of a bathroom. I found Elizabeth's bedroom. On the bedside table was a telephone with speed dial options. The first button was for the police, the second was for the fire department and the third was Godiva Chocolates.

My partner Johnny and I visited Casa Kimberley, Elizabeth Taylor's Puerto Vallarta hacienda. Just before our visit, we enjoyed some local cuisine. The food raced through my digestive system and I was forced to ask the tour guide for the nearest baño. She quietly motioned me aside and whispered, "We never let anyone in here," indicating, "This was Liz's private bathroom." I entered the pink room and perched. After Montezuma had his revenge I sat and pondered, "Gee. This is where Liz sat!"

If the Shoe Fits, Buy Two Thousand

JoJo Juan, Miss Manila summoned me to the Philippines where I was invited to an extravagant party at the palatial home of Imelda Marcos. Shortly after I found the piano, Imelda found me. She wanted to sing her favorite song, "As Time Goes By." Let me tell you ... Imelda Marcos can't sing or maybe her shoes were just too tight.

Later that week I attended an event honoring Imelda Marcos at the Manila Hotel. It was a bad day. The taxi driver who picked me up assumed that I was a stupid American and took me for a long joy ride through town. When we pulled up in front of the hotel I told him that I needed to go inside to get change. I reported the driver for fare gouging to the front desk and the police arrived and arrested him. Imelda was four hours late and I thought, "To hell with her," and left. When I exited the hotel I began to walk around the neighborhood. A short distance from the Manila Hotel I witnessed a bank robbery. The ever-present city patrol armed with machine guns opened fire on the robbers, unreservedly obliterating them right in front of me. I puked, went back to the hotel and waited for Imelda.

Hell to the Chief

While George H. W. Bush was in office, he made a visit to Beverly Hills. I was playing piano at Jimmy's of Beverly Hills, which was host of the presidential luncheon. Before the event, the restaurant had to meet strict requirements. Everything from fire code to security was stringently monitored. Poor Jimmy Murphy, the owner, wasn't prepared for the disruption. Walls had to be taken out; hallways and fire escape routes had to be expanded. One-third of the chairs, tables, and miscellaneous furnishings had to be removed. The real ass-kicker was when Jimmy found out "Jimmy's of Beverly Hills" was not in Beverly Hills ... it was in Los Angeles. Things were never quite the same at Jimmy's from there on. Thanks a lot, George!

Don't Cross Your Legs

Whenever Phyllis Diller found me at the piano, I would play her song "Here's that Rainy Day." She would go into a trance ... funny Phyllis left and "Melancholy Mama" stepped in. Many people don't know that Phyllis was a concert pianist—or that she loved gin. She sat with me one night at the piano at a Beverly Hills bash, and when she was pulling herself closer to the keyboard, she grabbed hold of the piano lid, which came slamming down on my hands. She squawked out a laugh and said, "Well, there goes your career."

She amassed a fortune but joked that she spent the bulk of it on plastic surgery. One of the funniest things I ever heard her say was "I've had so much plastic surgery, that if I cross my legs my mouth snaps open!" Phyllis always wore white gloves in public "I have so many liver spots I should be served up with a side of onions."

I had recorded my comedy album before she died, and called her to see if I could cop her trademark line, "Phyllis Diller is a very funny lady." She also suggested, "Jere Ring is a very funny man."

Free Tickets

Barbra Streisand recorded her third live album *One Voice* at a benefit concert at her Malibu home. Tickets were priced at $1,000 apiece. My dear friend Phyllis Morris just happened to have a beach house right next door to Babs. So on the night of the concert, Phyllis had scaffolding erected along the common privacy wall bordering their properties. A sturdy platform was secured on top of the structure, and accommodated twenty-some chairs. Phyllis invited a selected group for dinner, and afterwards we all found our seats to enjoy the show. During her performance, Barbra became noticeably annoyed and sent one of her minions to Phyllis' front door. The household staff delivered the message that Barbra requested Phyllis cease the intrusion. Phyllis said, "Fuck her. A Jew never says no to free tickets!" And we enjoyed the rest of the concert.

Who Are You Anyway?

My friends Phil Housey and Dr. Bill Lane lived next door to the legendary director George Cukor on Cordell Drive in the Hollywood Hills. I made frequent trips to their house. On one visit Phil asked me if I saw Katherine Hepburn.

"Where?"

"Next door," Bill said. "She's living at George Cukor's house." I sprinted out the front door and across the property but Katherine Hepburn had already disappeared. From then on, every time I went to Phil and Bill's, I would drive slowly, peer over the low white wall and search for her. Then one day I spotted her in a scarfed straw garden hat picking roses. I parked my car at the curb and stood at the wall. I called her name, and she looked up, smiled and said, "Hello."

The elderly Katherine Hepburn walked with uncertain steps and had little to offer in conversation. I'm sure she could have cared less about who I was. Heck, she probably didn't even know who she was.

Look at Your Hair

Patty LaBelle was sweet to come to my grandmother's eighty-fourth birthday party. It seemed that I bumped into Patti everywhere while living in Los Angeles. Every time I saw her, she had a new wild-ass hairdo, and I would shout, "Gurl! Look at yo hair!" It stuck out here; it stuck out there. Rainbow colors everywhere!

Wanna Go On A Cruise?

Bob and Cindy Mills should be listed in the *Guinness Book of World Records* in the category of *Most Devoted Fans*. They have turned up with an entourage at nearly all of the venues that I have played since 1982. There is one particular story about the committed couple that I share as often as possible. Cindy winces whenever I embark on this amusing tale and it is for that reason that I am happy to share it with the world!

One evening over dinner, Cindy commented, "I would love to go on a cruise with you sometime when you are performing." I said, "If you go as my guest you can travel for free but you would have to sleep with me." She confidently responded, "I would rather sleep with you than I would my husband." I smiled and answered, "Funny, that's what he said!"

CHAPTER 19

Dare Where Angels Fear to Tread

Why can't I go through that door? What's on the other side that I am not meant to see? Take a chance! Step over the line! Go ahead and walk on the grass! Move the barricade, and drive on! You may never know what fabulously exciting adventures you may encounter when you ... *Dare Where Angels Fear to Tread!*

How Did I Know?

I headed to California when I was twenty-two. I knew that I had to get out of Indiana because my family and peers did not allow me to live my life as a unique and free spirit. To pursue a showbiz career, I needed to leave home. Driving alone across the country was terrifying, especially since I did not know where I was going to land, nor where I would live.

Me Ain't Shy!

After arriving in Los Angeles, California, it took me more than a month to find a fabulous place to live. And once I found it, I stayed there for seventeen years. I kicked Los Angeles in the ass.

My first job was at Eric Ross Men's Clothing in Beverly Hills. Bob Dylan, Nancy Sinatra, and Kenny Rogers became my regular clients. I familiarized myself with them, determining how I might fit into their lives and what mutual reward lie within. My method proved successful. Whenever I would see a celebrity, I did not hesitate to chase them down. Yet it wasn't their autograph that I was after. Rather I wanted to establish a personal connection. A perfect example was my relationship with Liberace … need I say more?

Charity Begins at Home

Fundraising is a difficult task. People tend to enter avoidance-mode you when you ask them for money. However, it depends on how you ask. Powerful people have great influence and draw. In 1988, President Ford and his wife Betty joined me as honorary chairpersons for a fundraiser that I hosted for United Cerebral Palsy. Linda Evans, Joanna Carson, and Nolan Miller served on the board. The celebs did not volunteer for the event. I had to use my persuasive personality to court them, requiring a step-by-step process where I pursued a progression of connections. We raised over a hundred thousand dollars for the foundation.

Don't Walk on the Grass

I often walked the pathway to the top of the shoreline cliffs of La Jolla. On this particular day I noticed an inviting grassy knoll. Yet posted signs warned *Dangerous Area. Stay off Grass.* It didn't look dangerous to me, so I went to check it out. When I reached the far edge of the knoll, the dizzying height caused me to drop to my knees. I am terrified of heights and, in this instance; had to belly-up, slithering like a snake to the side of the cliff to catch a glimpse of the view below. As I was taking in the dramatic view, a woman in a white bathing cap caught my attention. She was flailing her arms and yelling for help. I jumped to my feet and ran to find a pay phone, and within minutes police and lifeguard vehicles arrived. Two strapping lifeguards dashed to the top of the cliff, quickly surveyed the situation, and jumped. The woman was not alone. She and her husband had been snorkeling and were caught in an undertow. While struggling to the reach the shore, her husband had a heart attack. The couple was pulled to the shore and rushed to the hospital. Had I heeded the signs and stayed off the grass, that day may have turned out quite different

Cobblers Who Could Have Been Governors

Dr. Elsa Colby-Morely was a noted clinical parapsychologist, a doctor's doctor. She treated CEO's of major corporations and heads of state. Metaphysically she could get into people's heads and had a keen awareness of the paranormal. She sat in my audience for a number of years. Elsa always came in wearing a print housedress and thongs. Her hair was died Nehi Orange. Intense ice-blue eyes looked right through you, and she was surrounded by an aura of explosive energy. Elsa chose me as one of her subjects for a study titled "Cobblers Who Could Have Been Governors"—in other words, those who are laying pipe or selling shoes that could in actuality be running our country. She predicted that I would be exceedingly successful. I believed her.

We were having lunch in Beverly Hills. A partition separated a row of booths, obscuring the view of neighboring diners. Midway through the meal, Elsa began exhibiting signs of discomfort. Her face became painfully contorted, and when I expressed my concern she responded, "Someone is desperately unwell in this room." At that moment her body jolted and she slumped into the booth. From the other side of the partition a woman yelled, "Someone call 911!" The man sitting directly across from Elsa on the other side of the partition was hit with a massive heart attack. He was dead on the floor.

There *Is* a Difference

I'm not religious. I'm spiritual. When Mamaw used to pray with my brother and me at bedtime, she would say, "May Lawrence take his family to church not because he feels he has to but because he wants to." Every week my family attended Sunday school, morning worship, and church again on Sunday night. When I was six years old, Pastor Kauffman called me to the front of the church to play "How Great Thou Art" for the congregation. I couldn't remember how it went so I played "Alley Cat" instead. That was the first time I played piano for an adoring audience.

I liked going to church. My favorite part of the sermon was when the pastor said, "Shall we pray…" I was baptized but I didn't know what it meant. Peer pressure inspired me to go forward and accept Jesus as my personal savior. I never really wrapped my brain around that one either. It wasn't until I was invited to join the Sanctuary Choir at Second Presbyterian Church in Indianapolis that I truly felt spiritual. It was in the music.

When I began to travel the world I was introduced to other cultures and their religions. Johnny made an observation when he and I were shopping at an open market in the streets of Kuala Lumpur. He pointed out that within one block of where we were standing there was a Buddhist Temple, a Synagogue, a Mosque and a Christian Church, and all the people from those houses of worship were shopping and commingling together in the streets.

Since I moved to California I had been on a continuous quest to find a church home. It took me thirty-two years to find the Palm Springs Presbyterian Church. The congregation is a friendly bunch and all-inclusive. Pastor Christine is a hippie love child, Jesus-goes-to-Woodstock kind of gal. She shoots from the lip and sends us away with inspiration and strength each week.

I pray often and I see God in everything. Mountains. A tree. Johnny. My dogs. I feel the presence of spirit, and I follow its lead. I surround myself with light. I consider Jesus, Mohammed, and Buddha to be representatives of the higher power that we call God. Moses, John the Baptist, and Brigham Young were spiritually moved. They all just happened to be in different parts of the world. While belief systems are divided, spirituality remains universal. God is just way too big to fit into one religion.

Start Writing

Everyone is writing a book. I had been talking about it for ten years. Mom and I were watching Jeopardy one night when Alex Trebek asked a $250,000 winner what he was going to do with the money. The contestant replied, "I'm going to finish my book."

Mom turned to me and said, "Why don't I just give you your inheritance now?"

"Why?" I asked.

"Your book. Don't talk about it, just do it!"

CHAPTER 20

My Greatest Performance

"Embrace the journey, keep your scope wide, and the experience will prove to be provident." The influence of the prevailing phrase set the stage for ... *My Greatest Performance!*

Life Is Good

In the spring of 2011, my partner Johnny and I were enjoying the beautiful early mornings at the dog park. My career was in a lull. Having grown weary of performing, I tapped my design abilities and began staging multimillion-dollar homes. I took pleasure in hours of gardening and swimming in the pool. One phone call changed all of that ...

How Could This Be Happening?

I flew to Indianapolis on Memorial Day, May 30, 2011, for a short visit. For some unknown reason, I had a nagging feeling that I might be staying longer than I had planned. My brother and his wife were attending a convention in Tampa, Florida. His eldest son was leaving for a medical mission in Haiti and the youngest was living in Pittsburgh. My eighty-seven-year-old mother was scheduled for a simple throat procedure on June 1, and all members of my tiny family were going to be out of town. The plan wasn't necessarily intentional. It just happened that way.

Mom's surgery went smoothly. The advancement in medical science allowed her to go under the knife at 9:00 a.m. and return home to her own bed later that afternoon. I was well informed of the responsibilities of post surgical care and was told that we would be contacted Friday morning with an assessment. When the hospital called a day early, I became alarmed. I knew that it was something serious and when they refused to give the results over the phone, I determined that the only thing that it could be was cancer.

Cancer sucks! A family friend once alleged that anyone who lives long enough is bound to get cancer. My partner Johnny refers to it as the body's rust. However you consider it, cancer sucks! I split down the middle when my mom was diagnosed with stage four throat cancer. My dear sweet mother had to hold me and console me. As if I had reverted to childhood, I sobbed as she rocked me on the edge of her bed. My eighty-seven-year-old mother still cared so much about me, her chubby little baby, that she attempted to wrap her arms around me and stroked my thinning hair. I was more devastated by the news than she was, and she was the one with the cancer!

In that intimate moment, I realized that I had to stay in Indianapolis. The thought of flying back to Palm Springs and leaving my mother to deal with the grim situation on her own was out of the question. I had no other choice but to put my design career and my life on hold. My partner Johnny's immeasurable love and support comforted me. He selflessly assured me that he would be able to manage our house, dogs and keep my life in Palm Springs going in my absence. Johnny is a survivor. That's why I love him.

Maladies … Yuck!

I was never fond of hospitals. I still prefer not to discuss maladies. I was as unfamiliar with the medical field and terms as I was with the rules of football. We took Mom to the Simon Cancer Center at the Indiana University Hospital in downtown Indianapolis for a second opinion. There we met with an otolaryngologist who referred us to a radiologist who introduced us to an oncologist. We set up scheduled appointments for radiation treatments and chemotherapy. For the next three months we made daily trips to the clinic. Thirty-seven concentrated radiation treatments were ordered. Throughout the treatment, I met with twenty-seven doctors. At first the daily trips to the cancer center were effortless, but after a few weeks they became taxing. As the grueling schedule continued, the radiation and chemo took their toll. Mom was a proud woman. For as long as she could, she carried on her routine of waking early, putting on makeup, dressing, and making herself attractive for the day. She was a classy lady.

She was also strong. Years prior, Mom and Dad celebrated their sixtieth wedding anniversary shortly before his death on December 21, 2009. Three days after his funeral, I reluctantly returned to Palm Springs. Mom bravely stayed on her own from that time forward. She quickly acclimated to her new life, and with my older brother's help she learned how to maintain business and investments. She never outwardly mourned the loss of her husband. Rather she channeled her feelings into personal strengths. Her force was my inspiration.

I was also becoming more aware of her wicked sense of humor, which only she and I shared. During my thirty-seven years of living in Southern California we spoke on the phone multiple times every day. She knew my inner most thoughts and intuitively recognized my emotions. We were more than connected. I was both son and daughter to her. We had an inimitable bond.

What Am I Doing?

I busted through the brick wall. I began cooking, cleaning, changing linens, assuming all household chores. Mom and I quickly fell into a pattern. Meals and medications stuck to a strict time line, and somewhere in between I made an effort to get Mom outside at least once a day—grocery shopping, a trip to the bank, or even a short drive. Church on Sundays was a given. Evenings were Wheel of Fortune, Jeopardy, and bedtime.

Once I adjusted to the routine, it became somewhat easier. My greatest challenge at that point was dealing with my situational depression. Living with a dying mother was catastrophic. I was homesick, missing Johnny and our dogs. My brother said, "This is only going to get worse, before it gets better." I couldn't imagine things getting any worse ...

Ain't We Got Fun!

For a period of time Mom did very well and was taking the treatments better than she thought she would. Her enthusiasm for life was bolstered and she began to resume her normal activities. The pace picked up and we went everywhere and did everything and laughed all the way. We started going out to luncheons and dinners, garden club meetings, and even made a trip to the Super Bowl Village. We were loving life!

Hold The Elevator, Please

The Columbia Club is a premier private club located on Monument Circle in Indianapolis that was originally formed by Benjamin Harrison in 1889. White marble floors, dark wood paneling, an imposing fireplace, and Tudor accents augment the stateliness of the lobby. The grand piano, which Hoagy Carmichael played in the club in the 1920s, is fully restored and graces the lounge just outside the Harrison Room, the club's award winning restaurant. My brother is on the board of directors and served as the club's vice president. So he made special arrangements for Mom and I to have dinner there. Following a great meal, we made our way to the cabaret on the third floor. When the elevator doors opened, I was excited to see one of my favorite servers passing and rushed out of the elevator to grab her. As Barbara and I embraced she looked over my shoulder and said, "Jere, you left your mother on the elevator."

As the elevator door closed I dashed to press the button but was too late. I pushed the button again, and the door opened. There stood my exasperated mother with hands on her hips.

Barbara looked at me and said, "I bet your brother wouldn't leave her on the elevator."

"No." Mom responded, "His brother would leave me at home."

And You'll Still Be Ugly

Mom loved to shop at Meijer. She always said, "They have the best prices in town!" When cottage cheese was on sale she would buy four or five at a time. On one visit, we were grabbing them by the armfuls when a trendy looking man standing nearby said, "You should try the organic cottage cheese. It's much better for you."

I leaned in front of him, looked at the price sticker, then at him. "At $5.19 for half as much? I'll stick with the stuff on sale."

"Well, you do look like you enjoy a juicy cheeseburger now and then," he snapped.

Mom glared at him, and retorted, "Well, he can always lose weight, and you'll still be ugly." *Wow!*

When we arrived at the checkout, Mom was getting pushy. I held up a brick of cheese and said, "Tell me if it hurts when I hit you with this." She came back with "Tell me if it hurts when I run over you with this shopping cart." The cashier held up a greeting card and asked, "Do you need a bag?" To which I replied, "No. I've got her."

The Monan Trail

The Monan Railroad, built in 1847, was transformed in 2003 when railways became greenways for recreational use. Mom and I were frequent visitors. I would set Mom in her wheelchair, and off we went on a four-mile trek (two miles out and two miles back) along the scenic pathway.

On one occasion, Mom asked, "Does this make you tired?"

"Yes," I said, "sometimes it does." Then I offered her a deal. "Why don't you push me up, and I'll push you back?"

There would be no more trips to the Monan.

The Trailing Arbutus Garden Club

Gardening was next to godliness with Mom. After a long absence from her friends, we made a spontaneous road trip to southern Indiana to join up with Mom's garden club buddies at a tour of the Oliver Winery gardens. When we arrived, "the flock of hens" were focused on the tour guide at the edge of a path. As we approached the group, one of the women turned around and caught sight of Mom, who was occupied opening her parasol. The woman grabbed the arm of a woman next to her and a chain reaction followed as the whole group left the tour to flock around Mom. Unaware that her entire audience had departed, the guide continued with her spiel.

Shortly after that, my partner Johnny came to Indiana for a visit. We were in front of the house taking in the beauty of the knock out roses. As we were standing in silence, Johnny all of a sudden walked back to the house, opened the front door, and yelled. "Annette, get your trailing arbutus butt out here and dead head these roses!"

Mom was obsessed with another flowerbed in front of her house. She was constantly nagging me to pull the weeds and clean it up. I hated that particular flowerbed. One more she said that she wished it were just grass instead of a flowerbed. "You want grass? I'll give you grass!" I borrowed my nephew's pickup truck and went to a north side nursery to purchase copious quantities of sod. I leveled the bed and lovingly replaced it with beautiful green grass. To this day whenever anyone asks about my love life I tell them that the he only thing I've laid in years is 600 square feet of sod in mom's front yard!

Friends

I never realized how popular Mom was or how many friends she had. She maintained a number of these friendships for more than sixty years. When her friends heard that Mom was unwell, they called to offer help and prayers. She received hundreds of cards, so many that I created what I called "The Wall of Fame."

One of the many friends who came to see Mom was Alvia Bernadette Catherine Lewis. Before I found my direction in life, Alvia was my college sweetheart. My family loved Alvia as much as I did. Twenty years ago, we had visited Alvia and her husband Dan at their home in Frankfurt, Indiana, to see their new baby. As I cradled the child in my arms, Mom said, "Just think … that could have been yours." With a grimace I replied, "I don't think so."

The day before Mom died, Alvia came to the house. Mom immediately recognized her by voice. It was a spiritual moment that neither Alvia nor I will forget. As a result, our friendship was rekindled. I am her vicarious husband while she has three of my vicarious children. We remain a happy family after all!

Storm Warnings

Foreboding clouds were filling the sky. The weather reports warned that severe thunderstorms were moving in. I was working at our mortuary on the north side of Indianapolis. Mom called me on my cell phone asking me where I was, and what time would I be home. When I told her it would be several hours, she asked which room she should go to if the storm became severe. I replied, "I would go into the pantry because it's in the center of the house."

"Well, things may fall on me in there," she said.

"Well, that's the idea!" I laughed. Mom wasn't amused, so I went into my brother's office and asked, "Where should Mom go if the storm gets bad?" He suggested the guest bathroom. And then said, "I told my wife to stand on the roof."

Moving Sideways Across the Bottom

Mom's throat cancer metastasized to her right breast, and on Wednesday, April 11, 2012, Mom had a mastectomy. I picked her up on a Thursday from the hospital. Friday night she went to a birthday party for a friend. On Saturday night we had dinner at the Columbia Club. By the time Sunday came around, she was unable to make it to church. That was a first.

At that point Mom's health started to decline. Her appetite waned, and she began to lose noticeable amounts of weight. As her steps grew shorter and less sure, she began using a cane. Our fun day trips were few and less frequent, as she preferred to remain resting at home. The smallest of things became greatly important to Mom: The small plastic drinking glasses I had purchased for the tap water she always carried with her, her special seat cushion, and her favorite blanket brought her much-needed comfort. Nurse Josie Jackson began to make biweekly visits.

Going Home

Because I planned to spend Christmas with the family, I decided to fly home to Palm Springs to be with Johnny for Thanksgiving. I needed the break, but I was uncomfortable leaving Mom. My brother and his wife had separated, and he had moved into Mom's house. The three of us lived in harmony, but many times my brother's demanding schedule precluded him from tending to Mom's needs. So before I left for Palm Springs, I made arrangements for Mom to have Life Alert, but she had very little time to use it. The Monday after Thanksgiving my brother called to tell me that Mom had taken a turn for the worse.

Altering my plans and flying home early, I entered the final phase. The paradigm had dramatically shifted. I slept on a sectional sofa in the den, which provided a direct visual of Mom's bedroom. I tied bells to a newly acquired walker, so that I could hear her if she got up to move about in the middle of the night. Within very few days, we found it necessary to admit her to the hospital. My family kept a common vigil until she was released.

Following Mom's release from the hospital, my brother left on a weekend business trip. I was certain that I could handle the situation, but I was wrong. I had to administer medications around the clock and monitor Mom's temperature every two hours. Just as my brother returned home, my mother's temperature spiked, and she went into convulsions. We rushed her back to the hospital, and I remained with her. I thought, *I have only so much time on earth with this woman. I'm not going to waste it.* From her hospital bed Mom suddenly made up her mind, "Disconnect all these things. I want to go home so that I can 'go home.'"

Whenever a baby is born at the Indiana University Hospital, a harp plays a gentle lilting melody over the general sound system. Everyone had left Mom's room, and I was readying for her discharge. Just as I was helping her into the wheelchair, we heard the baby song coming from the hallway. Mom looked at me and said, "Isn't that interesting? They're coming in and I'm going out."

On the drive home from the hospital, I took Mom by the various houses in which she had lived during her life in Indianapolis. She wanted me to call her ninety-five-year-old cousin, Thelma Reiger, in Cincinnati. I handed Mom the phone, and she said, "Thelma, it's Annette. I'm going to get there first."

Home hospice was initiated, and Mom spent her last days in a hospital bed. A steady stream of friends and family flowed in and out. Mom was non-responsive on her final day, still she knew we were there. Mom died in the late afternoon on Saturday, December 8, 2012.

My New Year's Resolution

I learned so much during the eighteen months that I spent with Mom. My father always said, "If you say you're going to do something, do it," and I did it. I went onstage, without rehearsal, and successfully performed as Mom's caregiver. I found my spiritual self. I have no regrets. My New Year's resolution was "to surround myself with people and circumstances that only enhanced my life." After all that I have been through, why would I allow anything else?

My mother is my spirit guide. She keeps me close to God. From now on, when the curtain goes up, I will be singing a new song.

CHAPTER 21

Encore

Time moves on regardless, of what we choose to do
With unknown opportunities, we live and muddle thru
A daily course of duties we strive to meet day's end
To awaken the next morning and do it all again.

But I discovered early on that life could be so grand
Not being solely satisfied with just what's in my hand.
I took that hand and opened doors that surely seemed to be
Obscuring untold treasure, waiting there for me.

I peeked through keyholes, cracks and jams to try to find a way
To open doors and windows but a price I had to pay
While searching every corner of a life that seemed to be
Consuming every ounce of strength and will instilled in me.

But once I found my footing, the pathway became clear
That I was meant to follow light and of darkness should stay clear.
Life's temptations lure us all to providence unknown
And sometimes when we land there, we think that we're alone.

But always know God speaks to all in loud but subtle voice
Allowing us to live our lives with advantageous choice
Of how to treat those less fortunate, their souls we must not spurn,
And from their meekness, we too ourselves can learn.

I know now why life's pattern once took me close to hell,
The demons bidding for my soul but I chose not to sell.
I found my way through tempest gale and rose to greatest height
And now am lifting others up so they may see the light.

We all start out with baby steps and as we grow we learn
That with each step, each stair, each path and each and every turn
In order to walk tall and sure, I want to say to you
If the shoe fits perfectly ... be sure you purchase two!

For all of you wankers who are complaining about not being mentioned in this book...

...Just wait for the next one!